LISTENING AND HELPING IN THE WORKPLACE

A guide for managers, supervisors and colleagues who need to use counselling skills

FRANK PARKINSON

A Condor Book
Souvenir Press (E&A) Ltd

First published 1995 by Souvenir Press
(Educational & Academic) Ltd,
43 Great Russell Street, London WC1B 3PA
and simultaneously in Canada

ISBN 0 285 63242 6

Printed in Great Britain by
The Guernsey Press Co. Ltd, Guernsey, Channel Islands

Contents

Preface

This book is not for the professional counsellor. It is for the welfare or personnel officer untrained in counselling, the junior manager, the supervisor, or indeed anyone in the workplace who may from time to time have to listen to a colleague in difficulty. It is also for anyone who wishes to learn more about some common human problems, how they affect the individual and those around him, and what the skills of listening can do to help.

It would be impossible in a book of this size to cover all of the problems that can arise in the workplace. But stress, redundancy, bereavement, trauma and bullying are particularly common, and I hope that my discussion of these issues will enable prospective listeners and helpers to glean the knowledge and understanding that they need in order to listen effectively. In addition, the Further Reading list (page 258) offers the opportunity to investigate particular interests.

The specific cases mentioned are based on real people and real incidents but, in order to protect the identities of those involved, names and some minor details have been changed. The term 'client' is sometimes used here to refer simply to anyone who comes with a problem and wants to speak to someone about it. It is not meant to label people as problems, or to distance one human being, the listener, from the other.

I would like to thank all those people from various companies and organisations who have helped in producing the ideas for this book, especially Caroline Gilchrist, head of counselling for W. H. Smith & Son Ltd, who helped to point me in the right direction.

Frank Parkinson

Introduction

People in positions of authority, whether managers, super-visors or other senior members of staff, are sometimes placed in a very difficult position by those for whom they are responsible. The same can happen to you as a colleague, workmate or partner. You may simply be working beside someone—perhaps you don't even know him very well—when he turns to you and begins to tell you his problems. What do you do? How should you react? What can you do to help? How do you remain objective—or should you get involved? Should you report it to someone else? What advice should you give? Should you give opinions or offer solutions? Is it helpful to be sympathetic, or should you be firm and positive? How do you listen when you have enough problems of your own, or feel that this per-son is wet, weak or stupid and that it's his own fault? It is probably inappropriate to think that you can help him to work right through his difficulties, even if you feel so inclined, but this does not mean that you should immediately refer him to someone else. The best way to respond is not likely to be:

> 'It's nothing to do with me. I don't know how to help. Go to the welfare officer.'

The thesis of this book is that most people can learn to help without becoming professional counsellors or trained helpers. Many problems are tackled and resolved at a fairly low level without ever coming to the attention of the professionals or even of managers and supervisors. If you are a junior manager or supervisor it is quite likely that someone will come up to you sooner or later and say, 'Can I have a word with you?' Before even thinking about referral—and to avoid the risk of sending the individual with the problem to the wrong person or agency—you will need to know something of the nature of the problem. You can do this through the art of listening, or what is sometimes called 'active listening'.

First we will examine the origins of workplace problems; we will look at some of the more common ones that either emerge from or find their way into the work environment. I will probably not be able to help, say, someone who has been bereaved unless I know something about bereavement and the process of grieving. Or, to take three more examples, how can I help the person in distress if I don't know what the trauma of marital misery, a divorce or an accident can do to him or her and to his or her family? So this book's first task is to offer information and some understanding of a series of problems and situations, so that the helper can begin to say, 'Aha! I have some idea of what this is about.' The three-stage approach to listening and helping, which will be discussed in Chapter 8, is based on a simple method which can be adapted to almost any situation. First, there must be some *exploration* of the problem and of what is happening now; then comes the creation of *understanding*, both in the 'client' and in the listener; then, eventually, the ability on the part of the client to take *decisions and action*. At its simplest:

What's the problem now, how did it arise, where should he go for help, what should he do?

We as listeners may not feel able to go very deeply into any of this, but we can all learn to respond in a more helpful and positive manner—by saying not 'What I think you should do is . . .', but 'Tell me more about that and what happened next.' Even those whose hearing is impaired can still listen via the use of sign language, lip reading and braille and by watching body language.

Some of the problems that arise in the workplace have their origins outside, either in the home or in the personality of the individual involved, or both. These can be personal, marital or family problems; problems with a partner or children; or financial or practical. Sometimes the workplace itself is a significant contributing factor—amongst the many causes can be the environment or colleagues, a supervisor or manager, sheer pressure of work or fear of redundancy. Whatever the cause, symptoms can range from mild to devastating and may need the services of a professional helper or counsellor. We can all, though, whether professionals or not, develop and extend our listening skills.

But learning to listen is not simple. It takes a great deal of energy and concentration to focus upon another person totally for any period of time, and a great deal of self-understanding and skill to be able to put aside our own prejudices, beliefs and opinions in order to help someone else to see and work through his or her problems—hopefully, in a new way. It is not easy to help him find the right direction so that he can begin to resolve his problems, as far as possible, in his own way. Neither is it easy to curb our own desire to give advice, opinions or instant solutions. It is hoped that this book will help many to understand what listening and helping are so that they will know both their own strengths and their limitations. On the one hand, we can *all* develop our understanding through listening; but on the other, we should know when we have done what we can, and recognise that the untrained person cannot do the work of a professional counsellor.

Most of us believe that we are good listeners, and we have all developed certain basic listening skills over the years. However, some find it easier to listen than others, while some feel that their job is to help people by telling them what to do. The process of listening is quite complicated, and real listening involves more than just hearing and telling. Communicating with others means that there must be a 'sender' and a 'receiver' of the 'message', each one having his or her own agenda which will influence both the sending and the receiving. Also, there can be many complicating factors, or blocks, between the two, and if we are to be good listeners we have to tackle the following questions:

- What lies behind the message, and how is it worded and transmitted?
- What unconscious meanings are being relayed through the way that the message is conveyed?
- What unspoken messages are being given out by each party through body language?
- How does the listener receive the message and interpret it?

And there are two basic questions that we need to ask ourselves:

1   What skills do we need as listeners and helpers?
2   What are we like, as people, when we listen?

We can consider these two questions in another way: the skills area is concerned with *doing*, and the personal area—the listener's nature and character—is concerned with *being*. In other words, what can we *do*, and how does what we *are* influence our listening and helping?

1   *Doing*—what can I do to help?
There is great emphasis in our society on doing—'Don't just sit there—*do* something.' Much professional training is concerned with this doing, and doctors, clergy, social workers and many other helpers must indeed 'do some-thing' to help their clients. But the desire to do, to help, can overshadow all else. For a start, people may *expect* us to do something about their problems, and often demand it:

'What are you going to do to help me?'
'I went to her and she didn't do anything.'

In line with this desire to help and the request for solutions, our response as helpers is to feel that we must act and be seen to be acting. Compassion requires us to do something so that the person who has the difficulty can go away feeling better. It also makes *us* feel better if we know that we have helped—perhaps the worst thing a helper can feel is that she hasn't been able to do anything. The trouble is that this very desire to do something can disable us and prevent us from doing what is most important of all—just being there, offering ourselves, and listening.

This immediately throws us back on to our main resource as listeners—ourselves—at the same time raising the question of what we are like as persons and how we respond to others. We need to be able to listen in order to understand—in other words, to 'stand under', to place ourselves under the umbrella of the other person's life and world. Listening is a function that attempts to focus on the person (or persons) concerned and on his or her total situation, including the here and now where the listening is taking place. In order to do this, as well as developing and extending the skills we already have, we need to learn certain basic techniques. Even when we have mastered the listening skills of prompting, mirroring, paraphrasing, reflecting, summarising and asking questions, we are still left with the problem of ourselves. And though we may have good responding skills, we may fail to be good listeners because our own blocks to listening get in the way. These blocks include prejudices, beliefs, experiences and feelings. Finally, we must look at our body language—what we do not say but show on our faces, the way we move, sit or stand, and other physical responses. Understanding these will help us to respond and listen at a deeper level.

2 *Being*—what do I bring to the situation?
Before we try to encourage or enable others to act, we need to know how we are likely to influence both what is happening now and what they will decide to do later. How do our prejudices and preferences affect what is happening between listener and speaker?

In what ways has my upbringing and background moulded what I am now? And how do these influence how I react and, therefore, to some extent, the decisions that the other person may make?

If I have been brought up to believe that people should be taught to stand on their own two feet and make the best of it, or if my parents were not very caring or loving, or if I have had difficult life experiences, I am likely to respond to someone with problems with such comments as:

'Pull yourself together and stop complaining. I coped, and so should you.'
'I know you are being made redundant, but I know plenty of people who have been through it and managed, so stop moaning about it and look for another job.'
'I've been married for twenty years and we've also had our problems. You just have to get on with it and make the best of it. You've just got to stick with it through thick and thin.'
'We had a baby that died so I know how you feel. You've just got to accept it and look to the future. That's what we did.'

These responses might sound helpful to the person speaking, but they do not look at the underlying problems of the person on the receiving end. They are centred on 'my' feelings and experience rather than 'yours'. I may be completely unaware of my own 'hidden agenda', of the fact that what I am hearing may be triggering reactions and feelings of mine that have little or nothing to do with the problem being presented to me.

How can you help if you don't understand? How can you understand if you don't first listen? How can you listen if you don't have the skills? How can you use the skills if your own personal agenda is getting in the way?

Both *Doing* and *Being* are inextricably bound up in the helping process.

Many voluntary helpers, supervisors, managers and ordinary workers are sometimes confronted with people whose problems are more serious than at first appears. Having imagined that they will be able to work through them, they may then find that they are getting into deep water. But this does not mean that those with no formal training in counselling or helping cannot help. Their presence alone, by showing that someone cares and is taking the time to be there and trying to listen, can make a great difference. You may not be a marriage counsellor, and you may not know much about debt problems or bereavement, but by using the skills described here, and bearing in mind that your task is not to solve the other person's problem for him, you will be able to respond appropriately, thereby enabling him to see his problems more clearly and to decide what to do about them; alternatively, you will be able to direct him to those best qualified to help.

Counselling and the listener/helper

The good listener and helper, who may not be a professional counsellor, uses the same basic skills as a counsellor in the process of listening and responding, but is not a counsellor. It may therefore help if we look at what is usually meant by the word 'counselling'. In some circles, it is associated with people either just listening and not responding, or with 'do-gooders' telling others what to do. It is also sometimes seen as something of a luxury provided by middle-class people who do not know what real life is about. In reality, counselling is neither of these things. At its most basic, it is an activity in which two or more persons participate, usually by choice. But it is not just confined to this pair or group: there can be much wider implications for the community and for society as a whole. Some see counselling as an individual and private matter, whilst others see it as addressing problems that begin in the community or family, focus on one individual, and then radiate back into the community or family—thereby raising questions about social as well as personal responsibility. In other words if, for instance, a person has a marital problem, there will be implications for the partner, for any children involved and for the wider community, especially if the marriage breaks down.

It may be useful to see helping activity as of three kinds:

1 *Instrumental.* Helping or giving information. The direction of the communication can be seen as downwards, in that one person knows something that the other does not. 'Tell me the way to the post office, please,' can result in specific directions and information. I know where it is, and you don't. The trouble with this is that it does not take into account what lies behind the request to find the post office. Not that it is always necessary to know this, but if the person asking the question wants something not provided by the post office, then the listener may need to direct him or her elsewhere. In this exchange one person is giving something directly and directively to another.

2 *Personal.* The sometimes intimate encounter between someone in need and a doctor, priest, psychiatrist, counsellor or other professional; or between two friends or colleagues, at work or at home. What is happening here is a struggle for both to understand, to make some kind of sense of the situation, and to make decisions. The direction of the communication may be seen as largely horizontal—from one person across to another.

3 *Political.* Political as well as social and personal factors influence our lives from outside, and may cause problems. Many human situations result from policies, rules and regulations, from a system over which we have little or no control as individuals. Sometimes, in order to lessen or alleviate problems, we need to tackle these primary causes by working for change within the system.

The direction of the communication here is from below, with people trying to change or adjust the rules.

These three ways in which the helper operates—instrumentally, personally and politically—are in some respects separate, and yet they merge into each other. And at the non-professional level too they can all be part of the helping and listening process. You may be trying to bring all three into play: to give information, to listen carefully and try to understand the problems, to try to change or influence the system:

> John was constantly late for work and often in trouble because of it. He could not afford a car and relied on local buses, which were erratic and often late. Also, he was sometimes late home, which caused problems with his wife not knowing when he would arrive for a meal. He talked to his supervisor, and it was decided to ask if he could work 'flexi-time'. This meant that he could clock in whenever he wanted to, as long as he worked a certain number of hours in the week. The manager agreed to this—it fitted in with the routine—and the problems were resolved. However, the supervisor had had to listen very carefully and with great skill because, to begin with, John was quite distressed about what was happening and thought he would lose his job and, probably, his marriage. In listening, the supervisor used all three types of counselling: he gave information, he listened carefully, and he helped to adjust the rules.

Counselling can be defined as:

> A method or process that provides the right atmosphere in which a relationship of trust between two or more people can be developed. As a result of this, people are enabled to discover the inner strength or courage to find their own way through their problems.

It is the counsellor's task to build up a relationship of trust and, by using various techniques and listening skills, to encourage the client to find her own solutions. Counselling has also been defined as 'two or more frightened people in the same room'—and this includes the counsellor. This means that the counsellor does not sit there with all the answers already to hand, but he too experiences anxiety. There are many other definitions, but most are based on the belief that it is unhelpful and unethical to give advice or tell people what to do. You cannot help if you don't understand the problem, and the only potential expert is the person at the centre. No matter how much I try, I cannot stand in anyone else's shoes. And if I do attempt to solve their problems, it will be in my way and not theirs.

The basic question is: how deeply does the listener move, or is he able to move, into the problem? A trained psychodynamic counsellor, for instance, may take a person back to her childhood and look at problems in her relationship with her parents, then help her to work through the present reactions and emotions generated by the past. Such a counsellor may look at sexual or other problems in a relationship and find that hidden events and feelings are emerging and influencing present behaviour. He may use cognitive or behavioural techniques or a person-centred approach. These theoretical approaches should be used only by those trained in the appropriate models, methods and skills. If a non-professional counsellor or listener attempted to use them, he would almost certainly do more harm than good. However, what the non-professional *can* do is to learn to use listening skills. Remember that it is often sufficient to provide a listening ear in order for the other person to begin to see his own way through his problems:

A young sergeant caught the chaplain at the back of the garrison church and asked if he could talk to him. The chaplain was not a trained counsellor, but had learned listening skills. They sat down and for over an hour the sergeant talked. The chaplain was unable to speak because the sergeant talked all the time. All he did was to try to listen and hope that he was saying 'Yes' and 'Uh uh' in the right places. Eventually the sergeant stood up and said, 'Thank you, Padre. You've been a great help to me.' The

Padre hadn't said a word after 'Tell me why you've come', except to respond at a minimal level. But just by talking to someone who was willing to listen—not counsel—the sergeant was able to work out what he had to do.

A listening ear should never be underrated.

Counselling is a helping and enabling activity conducted by someone who is trained, usually to use a particular model and method, or, sometimes, a combination of methods. It usually takes place within a particular cultural or organisational context with certain accepted ways of working or behaving, and can be with an individual, a couple or a group. Most counselling models and counsellors do not offer advice. In fact an ex-director of counselling for Relate said that advice should be kept in a bottle marked 'poison'. Counsellors may give information, but the direction this takes and how it is used are left to the counsellor.

Good and effective listening is essential to the counselling process and is the art of being able to focus totally on what another person is saying. The listener attempts to discover why this is being said, what it means, where it comes from and what lies within, behind and underneath it. Good listening is an active process which involves an awareness of what is being said, but also of what is not said, but may be expressed through behaviour and body language.

The listener need not be a trained counsellor, but will use the same listening skills as a counsellor.

Listening effectively is therefore not simply a matter of learning new skills, but of developing the skills we already have. My hope is that this book will enable non-professional helpers to learn to listen effectively, not only in the workplace but wherever they find themselves.

PART ONE:
PROBLEMS IN
THE WORKPLACE

1 Where Do Workplace Problems Originate?

Wherever there are people—and this includes the work-place—there will be problems. There will be personal problems generated from within individuals, groups, families and communities; problems created by the interaction between the work environment and the individual or group; problems resulting from the interchange between individuals and groups at work. These problems can have many causes and be of many different kinds. Those who attempt to listen to and help others in the work environment must be aware of the complexity of causes and effects as they influence people and emerge as problems. Rarely is any problem as simple as it seems, for we often do not know where it begins or what the causes are, or what the wider effects may be.

We can draw three overlapping circles (Figure 1), one representing the individual, the second the home environment and the third the workplace. All three are interlinked in a pattern that changes, depending on the circumstances of each at any given time. Sometimes the overlap is greater in one part of one of the circles than in the others. Personal or individual problems may invade the circles of home or work. Sometimes home life produces the main difficulty, and this intrudes into relationships and performance at work. At other times, problems at work make for difficulties at home or deterioration in personal health. Depression may be the result of stress at work or of the breakdown of a relationship at home, or it may be the result of chemical changes in the

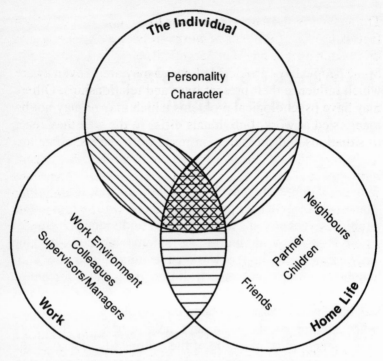

Figure 1.   The individual—home—workplace.

brain or nervous system. Problems in any one area can cause problems in the others.

1   IN THE INDIVIDUAL

There are many factors within an individual that make for problems in the workplace, depending on the character and experience of the person concerned. Some may have problems that are deep-seated, deriving from past experiences—from their birth and childhood—while others' difficulties may seem to have developed from later events. And here the old 'nature—nurture' argument also comes into play: are people the result of what they are born with genetically, or of their upbringing and later life experiences?

The answer is similar to the answer to the question of which factors produce problems at work—it is not necessarily just this factor or that one, but can be all, or in this case, both. Some people have problems of which they aren't even aware which influence their present lives and relationships. Others may have psychological problems which may or may not be manifested at work. Individuals differ in the way they react to situations and pressures: in response to stress, some are fairly relaxed and find it easy to cope, while others seem 'up-tight' and may become angry or aggressive; some are able to relate to others in a confident manner, are outgoing and extrovert, while others are shy and introvert, quiet and retiring; and some are just difficult. Whatever the causes, personal and personality problems will intrude into and affect life both at home and at work.

2   IN THE HOME

Where do home problems originate? Some are the result of personal and personality factors, and others stem from an unhappy working environment and unsatisfactory conditions. But some problems originate in the home itself and find their way into work. It is difficult, if not impossible, to say what the real causes are and where the roots of any specific problem lie:

- Is it the unsuitable working environment, or that these particular people don't get on together, or that this individual is having problems in his marriage?
- Is it that she can't seem to relate to and get on with her colleagues at work, or is it that her teenage children are on drugs and in trouble with the police, or that her partner is an alcoholic, or that a parent or friend has just died?
- Is it that there is too much stress at work, or that her husband has just been made redundant, or that he can't cope with the stress of having a new baby in the house?

- Is it that she just can't cope at work, or that she is on the verge of a nervous breakdown because of an impossible home life?

The factors in each case are probably all interrelated, but when a problem originates in the home and then arises at work, it may show up in different ways:

- I become irritable and difficult at work because I am having problems in my marriage and have had a row with my partner.
- I can't seem to cope with my work and I've become depressed, but it may be because I am having financial problems. My husband has just been made redundant and we won't be able to pay the mortgage or maintain our present standard of living.
- I suddenly burst into tears or become morose, and feel isolated and will not talk to anyone, and nobody seems to know what's wrong with me. I am a single parent and am having problems with my two children, and their father will not contribute towards their upkeep.
- I am not working as efficiently as I usually do and my performance has dropped. My boyfriend has left me and I have just discovered that I am pregnant and my parents want me to leave home.
- I become angry and aggressive at work and sometimes burst into tears for no apparent reason. I am single and live at home with my mother who is seriously ill and I have to cope with her when I get home.
- I don't seem to enjoy my work and I isolate myself from my workmates. I have just found out that my husband is having an affair and feel ashamed and angry.

So problems from home can produce anything from difficulties at work and in personal relationships with colleagues to depression, stress and illness. I may be going through a divorce; it may be a question of alcoholism—mine or that of someone else in the family; it could be drugs; it may be the children, or a parent, or an impossible neighbour; it could be sexual problems or other difficulties in my relationships; it could be debt or some other financial problem; it could be some kind of bad news. All of these, and more, can originate in the home and influence behaviour at work.

3   IN THE WORKPLACE

Some problems are the result of the work environment. People working in coalmines may suffer because of unhealthy conditions and develop respiratory diseases such as pneumoconiosis, asbestosis or silicosis. Some working in factories may suffer from extreme boredom and lethargy because of monotonous procedures and practices and feel a strong sense of isolation or lack of purpose. Even the colour and decor of an office are said to cause people to feel either good and positive about their work or depressed and sad. Eyesight problems can result from staring for long periods at word processor monitors or at the screens of computer systems, and RSI (repetitive strain injury) is now a recognised medical condition. Open-plan offices may contribute to workers feeling that they are just numbers in an impersonal system or that they exist in pigeon-holes or in cells in a beehive and have no privacy or separate identity.

Research into industrial illnesses has resulted in laws to control working conditions in order to reduce the risks of physical or mental disorders. The aim of employers and employment laws should be to create good working conditions, where people feel valued and where they can work as comfortably as possible in an environment conducive to good health and efficient production.

Other workplace difficulties stem from personal problems that happen to occur in the workplace, for it is impossible to create conditions that will prevent people from disagreeing with each other or from having problems in their personal relationships. Two people working at the same desk, counter or bench may have opposing views on religion, politics or any other topic. One may complain about the other; they may just 'get on each other's nerves' or intensely dislike each other. One person or group may make life intolerable for another. There can be problems between rival groups, or between those in management positions and those who are managed. These can be personal problems, or problems resulting from the system or organisation, or from the attitudes or misconceptions of those at different levels in the managerial structure:

> In one area of the country, social work teams felt very strongly that 'those up there don't care about those of us who are at ground level. They exist for themselves and for the benefit of those above them.' They saw themselves as working 'at the coalface', whilst those above were looking after their own interests and promotion prospects. Within the teams there were a few who felt that others were not pulling their weight, and even when relationships were good there were often feelings of isolation and loneliness— 'I have my own problems at work, but I can't share them with my colleagues.' Sometimes this was not because the person concerned didn't trust or like them, but because he realised that his colleagues were already under great strain and didn't want to burden them further. In addition, there seemed to be a high level of divorce and other marital and personal problems outside work.

The difficulties these people experienced at work were a mixture of personal problems generated by their work and working conditions, and problems to do with the interplay of different personalities and coping methods and the stresses of the job, but with the addition of difficulties that they brought in from outside work. Here personalities, the home environment and the workplace were all interlinked.

The regulations within a system can also cause problems. Helpers and carers in many organisations may feel anger, frustration, impotence and guilt about the restrictions under which they work, especially when they are unable to assist someone who comes to them for help. There can be strong feelings of unfairness and injustice:

'Think what it does to me and how I feel when I am faced with someone who is destitute or homeless and I have to say I can't help her because she doesn't fit the rules.'

'Because of her problems I would like to give her some time off, but the rules don't allow me to do it.'

Sheer pressure of work and fear of redundancy can cause irritability, isolation, anger, fear, stress and illness. When the economic climate is difficult, there may be many people unemployed and organisations begin to cut back on staff and expenditure:

In one large firm there were twenty-four people in the customer relations department. Gradually the numbers were reduced to twelve and those remaining were sent on courses so that they could do the work of those who had been made redundant. People said, 'I am now doing the work previously done by two or three.' Unless the others are incompetent or not working very hard, it is physically and mentally impossible for one person to do the work of three—but it was generally felt that this was what was happening. The reality was that more pressure was indeed being put on those remaining. Stress and sickness levels increased, and the fear of redundancy meant that there was rivalry and jealousy and everyone was 'watching his own back', the previous feeling of solidarity and of team spirit having diminished. The managers were also under more pressure and had suffered redundancies. Pressure on both staff and management resulted in a frightened, disgruntled and angry workforce who felt little sense of belonging or loyalty. If they were sick they were threatened with dismissal, so they were frightened of being ill and, when they were, often went to work all the same, thus becoming more ill. So illnesses and stresses increased.

Human beings are not isolated individuals, but belong to families, groups, communities and societies. At work they meet other people in a particular and sometimes peculiar environment, and need to be able to relate to them and survive. It is not always easy to deduce whether a problem that manifests itself at work originates in the individual personality, in the home or in the workplace itself.

THE WORKING ENVIRONMENT

Where is your 'workplace', and what is it like? Is it inside a building or in the open air? Perhaps you travel from place to place by car or train. Do you drive a lorry or a taxi? Do you work in a shop or store, an office or a laboratory, on a farm or in a factory? The fact is that there are thousands of different kinds of jobs and thus many kinds of workplaces, and usually the workplace is not just one defined area where you are occupied for the whole of your working time. If you work in a factory, you do not just go to your bench and stay there until you leave. You will have a tea break and a meal break, and you may go to a canteen or restaurant. There will be car parks and staff rest-rooms, and perhaps sports and recreation facilities. Some workplaces even have a crèche for babies and children. Others organise committees and groups to raise money for charities and outside activities.

All of this means that the workplace is usually a place where you move around and at certain intervals take periods of rest. It is a place where there are rules about working conditions, with laws to determine work environments and facilities. Rarely is the workplace an isolated environment where there is no movement and no contact with other people. A long-distance lorry driver, for instance, should by law drive only for a certain length of time and then take a rest. There will be roadside cafés and lay-bys, motorway restaurants and rest areas, a pick-up point and place of delivery. All of these, for the driver, can be seen as the constituents of his 'workplace'.

To deal with a problem at work it may be necessary, as already mentioned, to look at many other areas of a person's life. I may try to help someone who is finding it difficult to cope at work, and the situation will be further complicated if that person is having marital problems, drinking too much or trying to face up to a bereavement. Sometimes serious problems of confidentiality arise. Some take the view that what happens at work and at home are two entirely separate areas and must be treated as such.

> Within the armed forces, it was once believed that what a soldier did at home was of great concern to his unit or regiment or, even, to the whole army. If a man had an affair with someone's wife, especially if from the same unit, he was usually moved elsewhere, sometimes within a matter of hours. The 'sunshine method' of dealing with welfare problems was very popular. A senior rank would simply take the soldier aside or into his office, grab him by the throat and say, 'Look here, sunshine, get yourself sorted out by tomorrow or you will feel the consequences!' Although there is still concern for individuals' personal responsibilities, there is much more concern about treating service personnel as people with the same rights as other citizens. Indeed, some would argue that as long as he does his job satisfactorily as a soldier, what he does outside work should be of no concern to the army or to anyone else.

The problem with this latter view is that it does not take into account the complexity of human life and experience. Sometimes problems *are* confined to one place, either home or work. But just as often they are not. The workplace, for instance, is not an area completely detached from all other parts of a person's life, any more than it is one 'place', static and immovable. Any attempts to help people who have problems must take this into account. Look again at the soldier. Does it matter if he is having an affair with someone else's wife? It does if he is walking in front of her husband on patrol. The same would apply in any civilian organisation where people work closely together and need to be able to trust and support each other. Within the armed forces the extramarital behaviour of senior officers has been highlighted recently by the media, new rules of conduct have been issued, and the pendulum may have started to swing the other way again. All of this means that we must include the 'human factor' when we talk about the workplace and have a dynamic view of what it is.

Neither is the workplace completely detached from the outside world. A GP has his consulting rooms in a house or medical centre, but he will make house calls and be in contact with hospitals and clinics. He will need to relate to patients, partners, other doctors, secretaries, midwives, district nurses, counsellors, medical representatives, his accountant and many different kinds of specialists. He will also be responsible for the practical and financial management of his practice. He may have a wife and children, friends and family, and many other interests in his life, all of which may be affected by his work, especially when he is on call or there is an emergency.

Similarly, an office worker has 'the office', but this can be anything from a conventional single room to a shoulder-level compartment in a large open-plan room with dozens of other people. It may be in a small complex or a large one, in the heart of the country with a magnificent view over park land, or windowless and in the centre of a large city. It may be a study at home, or a cubicle in a shop or store or in a purpose-built, high-rise block.

So the workplace expands in an ever widening circle to include even such places as rest-rooms, restaurants, staff rooms, toilets, corridors and lifts. Much depends on this environment. It is capable of creating feelings of contentment or feelings of confusion; an atmosphere of tension or stress, or an atmosphere of peace. It brings people into a wide circle of influence, from colleagues and work-mates, directors, managers, and supervisors, to welfare officers, personnel management and occupational health staff, cleaners, maintenance workers, clients, customers, occasional visitors and many more besides. Some consider work to be a vocation, while others see it simply as a means of earning money. But whatever the view of work or the reason for working, the workplace is always an extension of, a part of, our lives. It is often said that we shouldn't take work home with us, but some people have to, perhaps because they haven't the time to complete a task at work or because they have to prepare for the next day or for future developments. Teachers, for example, take home marking and have to plan their lessons and keep abreast of new information and materials, as well as the many changes taking place in the administration and performance of their duties.

It can be argued that, since our lives do not consist of separate compartments, we all take our work home in some way or other. The different parts are all interlinked and make up our total experience of living. If I have been under great pressure at work, it is difficult, if not impossible, to leave my work behind me and go home completely relaxed and at ease with the world. I may express my anger and frustration with my partner, family and friends by being irritable; alternatively, I may be quiet and withdrawn. I may even resort to 'kicking hell out of the cat'. Or, more seriously, I may become violent towards my wife and family or become ill and depressed. If, on the other hand, I have been promoted or given a pay rise or have simply had a particularly successful day at work, I will probably come home elated, generous and loving.

What I do at work becomes part of who and what I am. The effect can be helpful and positive, or destructive. The idea in 'attachment theory' is that as we grow and develop, from birth, we attach ourselves to objects and people, places and things and they become part of us and therefore part of our lives. Our work, whether transient or long-lasting, influences every part of our lives. The trouble is that the workplace is often a constantly changing environment where we have to meet and relate to other people—another potential cause of strain and stress. And although we may have strategies for coping, these are not guaranteed to leave us cool, calm and collected.

One method used by some people to cope with the stress of their work is to shout and swear while driving home in the car—often to the amusement or consternation of other drivers. Others listen to music or put their energies and frustrations into sport or hobbies. Others become quiet, isolated and introvert.

The effects of the interaction between the workplace, the personality and other problems can sometimes be quite destructive, even devastating:

> Mary worked filling shelves in a supermarket. Not a very skilled or stressful job, some would say. She should just go to work, do the job and take the money—no worries. Easy. But she had a supervisor who, for some unknown reason, didn't like her and often gave her the difficult and urgent jobs to do, putting Mary under great pressure and stress. The slightest mistake would result in anger and criticism and the threat of dismissal. 'If you can't cope, there are plenty out there who can', was the ultimate threat. After work, feeling tired, angry and humiliated, Mary would travel home, where she would cook meals, do the washing and ironing and housework and care for her husband and three teenage children, all of whom expected her to be at their beck and call. Although her small income was essential for their household finances, her husband thought of her work not as a means of bringing in extra money, but as a kind of hobby and not a 'proper job'. Mary was always tired and listless and gradually became unresponsive at home and uninterested in her family. At work she began to make more and more mistakes and suffered further criticism and pressure, which intensified all her problems. Eventually she went to the doctor suffering from stomach pains, headaches and depression. She felt that she couldn't cope either at work or at home.

It is sometimes extremely difficult for people to cope with particular incidents:

> James, a policeman, had to attend a serious road traffic accident where two people were killed, one a small child.

He had seen dead bodies before, but not that of a child. At the time he was horrified, but he pushed his feelings down inside, coped and got on with his job. When he returned to the police station, his inspector passed him in the corridor and asked him how he was. He said, 'I'm all right, thank you, sir', and carried on. That night he hardly slept, and the image of this young child kept coming into his mind. For almost a week after the accident he had nightmares and would get up in the middle of the night and go into the bedroom of his own young daughter and check to see that she was still breathing. He often became very emotional at home, at one moment feeling angry and upset and then being withdrawn and silent. His wife couldn't understand what was happening, and became annoyed when he woke up in the middle of the night sweating and frightened.

Unfortunately James met with little understanding either at home or at work, and gradually he began to suffer from post-traumatic stress. This resulted in long periods of time off work, and eventually required the services of a clinical psychologist to whom he was referred by the occupational health nurse.

Jane is a typical example of the individual whose problems at home create difficulties for others at work:

Jane's marriage was breaking down after fourteen years, and she knew that this was causing tensions in the office. She spoke to her line manager and supervisor, Margaret, who didn't know what to do other than suggest that she go to Relate for marriage counselling. Margaret was aware of the problems caused by Jane's mood swings and bouts of anger or silence, but she didn't know what to do about it. Should she report it to her superiors? This was difficult, especially as Jane had come to her in confidence and asked her not to tell anyone. Because of the feelings generated within the team and Jane's difficult behaviour the atmosphere was often tense and volatile. This lowered morale and sometimes resulted in poor performance and low output generally. Also, some had complained to Margaret and asked her to do something about it. So she was torn between trying to understand Jane's problems and the reasons for her behaviour, and realising that she could not let the situation remain as it was or wait until it became worse. Because her own marriage was stable and happy she didn't really understand why Jane behaved as she did. Her instinct was to give her an official verbal warning, although she tried to sit and listen to her whenever she came to see her. But she had no counselling or listening skills training and found it very difficult to cope with her own feelings. Eventually she persuaded Jane to go to see the welfare officer, and this was the beginning of a long process of counselling.

The problems would have been exacerbated had Jane turned to alcohol or drugs—which sometimes happens in such situations.

Problems in the workplace have many different and possible origins and often these are interrelated. They may be from a person's background and personality or generated at home or in the working environment. These three areas, the personal, the home and the workplace, are not separate, and what happens in one can, and invariably does, influence the others.

It is therefore necessary for the listening helper to understand the nature of these influences and their effects on an individual and others within the workplace.

2 Stress

Stress is a common problem, not only in the workplace, but also in life in general. To be stressed is normal—to be alive is to be stressed. The fact that the heart is beating and pumping blood around the body creates stress. Breathing, moving and even relaxing cause some element of stress. Without it we would not drive safely, stand up for ourselves, survive in relationships or do our work efficiently and effectively. It is often said that someone is off work suffering from stress, when what is really meant is that his stress level has increased to the point where he feels that he can't cope and he is experiencing disturbing symptoms. This is when stress become distress.

Throughout any given day our stress level and capacity to cope will vary. Putting this in the work context, when a person goes in to work in the morning her stress level probably increases, and then fluctuates throughout the day, depending on what happens. It may rise when a particularly difficult event occurs: an irate caller on the telephone, a summons from the boss, pressure to finish a job in a specified time; or when the noise level increases, a pile of mail or files arrives, a difficult customer has to be dealt with, an argument with a colleague arises or an accident happens. Similarly, stress levels can fall when there is a coffee, tea or lunch break, or when we feel that we are coping and working successfully. It would probably also fall if we were congratulated after a particularly satisfying piece of work, or our relationships with our colleagues had become especially positive. It would also be true to say that a rise in our stress level can often be good for us. If you

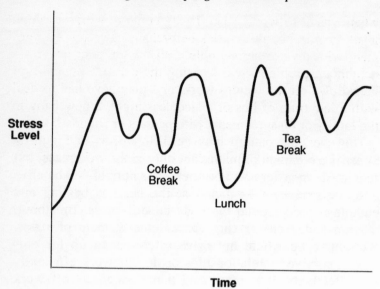

Stress
Level

Coffee
Break

Lunch

Tea
Break

Time

Figure 2. Normal stress level during the working day.

were told that you had been promoted, you would probably
be quite exhilarated and there might be a rise in your
heartbeat and a feeling of pleasure and achievement. This
could also be touched with feelings of anxiety at the new
responsibility that promotion will bring.

But, there is a point above which normal stress moves
into distress, and this point varies, not only from day to day
but from one person to another. I may cope with a difficult
job or situation one day and not the next, even though the
demands of work have remained the same. I may also cope
on days when my stress level has increased well above
what I would normally expect or experience. My coping
mechanisms may be better on some occasions than others.
In other words, our capacity to cope with stress is not set
permanently at one level. A normal stress level chart might
look like Figure 2. I go to work and my stress level rises. It
then varies throughout the day until I go home, at which
point my stress level may be either lower or higher than

when I went to work. Also, I may come to work at a high level, having had difficulties beforehand: perhaps an argument with my partner, trouble with the children or with a neighbour, problems with starting the car or a puncture or breakdown on the way to work; or I may have had to deal with a late train or bus or a sleepless night, a new baby in the family or disagreements with parents or friends.

However, the pattern may be different, as in Figure 3. When I go to work (point (a)), the pressure immediately increases, my stress level rises and I begin to work harder and exert more pressure on myself. I will probably begin to enjoy this and produce more and better work. Some people do work better under pressure and feel a sense of excitement and satisfaction. If the pressure continues, I work even

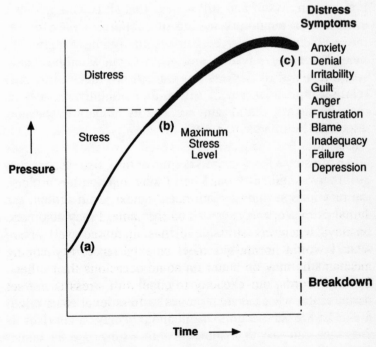

Figure 3. Distress level.

harder and reach point (b), where I feel the stress has reached a level at which I am beginning to find it difficult to cope. This is my 'maximum stress level'.

If the pressure increases from both outside and inside, I begin to experience certain symptoms. I may become anxious and worried, but may deny that I feel these things and say that I am not under pressure. I say that I can cope and ask people to leave me alone. But I begin to discover that I am not coping and feel a sense of frustration and anger both with myself and, perhaps, with those who have given me the work, or with the work itself. I become irritable and restless and the symptoms intensify. I may even feel ashamed and guilty that I am not coping and even more strongly try to convince myself that I really am coping. My ability to make decisions can be affected and I may experience difficulty in concentrating. I exert more pressure on myself and still believe that all is well, and may even have a temporary feeling of euphoria: I have moved into a kind of 'over-drive'. But eventually I have neither the mental nor the physical energy to cope. Gradually may come feelings of depression, inadequacy and failure. My relationships with others suffer, and although colleagues may be aware that I am not coping they are probably unable to help because I push them away in my anger and frustration.

As my stress level increases I move into distress, but may still deny it and carry on. I will probably experience physical reactions such as sweating, an increase in heartbeat and blood pressure, a dry mouth, tension and even pains in the chest. If the level continues to rise and I reach point (c), I will have reached a real crisis where I may become confused and irrational and, eventually, my mind and body refuse to carry on. We usually call this a 'breakdown', because the whole system ceases to function effectively. If I am aware of what is happening, or my supervisor or manager can see that something is wrong, I may take a break, have some time off or go home.

Factors at work that can raise stress levels

- Too much work, long hours, few breaks, too many cases and too many clients.
- Too little work, with a rise in boredom and conflict levels and a decrease in feelings of satisfaction.
- New rules and regulations, and insufficient time to absorb or adjust to them.
- New managers, supervisors or colleagues.
- Being made responsible without being given the necessary authority or compensation.
- Not having clear objectives or aims.
- Not being kept aware of what is happening—lack of information.
- Threat of redundancy.
- Low wages or a decrease in salary, especially when managers or others are given increases.
- Being undervalued through low pay or by other people.
- Being promoted; being demoted or simply not promoted, especially when others are.
- Seeing others dismissed or made redundant.
- Working with hostile, unhelpful or aggressive colleagues, managers, supervisors, clients or customers.
- Working with people who are uncaring, incompetent or lazy.
- Sexual harassment, intimidation or bullying.
- Constant interruptions.
- Inadequate heat or light or uncomfortable working conditions.
- High noise levels.
- Isolation—lack of contact with others.
- Increased demand—more work than can be coped with.

REACTIONS TO STRESS

People try to control their response to stress through a process of distancing themselves from the stressors. They try to do this by:

- Controlling their emotions by consciously suppressing them. They may fear that if they are not coping they may be seen as weak or inadequate.
- Denial that there *are* any stress-induced responses—'It isn't happening and I am coping.'
- Rationalisation: believing that 'It has to happen to someone and somebody has to do it—it's my job to cope.'

The result can be:

- An inability to sympathise with others. Some may become intolerant of colleagues, supervisors, family and friends.
- A refusal to talk about it, or talking all the time—'I don't need to talk', or, 'I've got to tell you all about it.' The talking may be about something other than the problem.
- Feelings of isolation and an inability or disinclination to meet or mix with others. Some will avoid contact with other people or situations and their emotional reactions may keep others away.
- Irritability and loss of temper; being generally uncooperative.
- An inability to concentrate and difficulty in making decisions. There may also be unusual and out-of-character impulsive actions.
- Feelings of anxiety and vulnerability. People will sometimes take things personally and take their problems home with them. This may result in sensitivity to noise, or difficulties with relationships, family, children, colleagues or work.
- Resurrection of problems from the past, which may come to the surface and interfere with the present.
- An inability to 'switch off' or relax; sleeplessness and being constantly tired and listless.
- Loss of any sense of humour; taking things too seriously.
- Feelings of anger and aggression.

- Changes in attitudes, beliefs and relationships. Someone may change and seem not to be the person that he used to be. He may change religious or political views and alter his lifestyle.
- A general dissatisfaction with work, family, home, colleagues, friends and life in general.

There can also be feelings typical of loss and bereavement. A sense of shock is common—'Why me?'—and denial that there is a problem. Anger, frustration and even violence, perhaps out of character, may result. There may be shame, regret or guilt, feelings of isolation, loneliness and rejection. Depression may set in, with feelings of sadness and a sense of pointlessness.

Signs of stress
Consider this self-check list of stress signs:

- Are you able to relax easily when you need to?
- Do you feel guilty when relaxing or trying to relax?
- Do you feel that you should always be doing something?
- Do you often lie awake at night worrying about things?
- Do you sometimes feel a tightness in your neck or chest and do you sometimes have a thumping heartbeat?
- Do you easily become irritated?
- Do you have disturbed nights?
- Do you make decisions easily and confidently?
- Would you describe yourself as a worrier?

If you answer 'yes' to some of these, then you may be experiencing a higher than normal level of stress.

COPING STRATEGIES

How can we prevent stress from moving into distress? There are a number of ways, which will vary from person to person:

1   Identify stressors
The first priority must be to ensure that potential stressors
and the signs of stress are identified and recognised. Try to
identify the sources of the stress.

- What are the external factors? Is it a person, group or
  situation? Is it a particular incident or event? Is it something or someone at work or at home?
- What are the internal factors? Is it something about
  you—an attitude, experience or disappointment, or a lack
  of fulfilment or achievement? Is it lack of appreciation
  from others, not feeling valued?
- What feelings are aroused in you by this? Shame, anger,
  guilt, regret, disappointment, depression, withdrawal,
  hatred, bitterness, fear, sense of isolation or pointlessness, lack of purpose?

Sometimes little can be done about the source of the
stress, but it may help if things can be changed—however
slightly—or adapted.

2   Be positive

- Be positive about your feelings and accept them as
  normal.
- Try to direct the feelings where and with whom they
  belong.
- Try to find a way of expressing how you feel. Some claim
  that swearing and shouting help to relieve tension and
  anger, although you may need to be careful where you do
  these.
- Are your feelings directed at the wrong person or people?
- Can you do anything to change the situation, and can you
  speak positively to those involved?

3   Be assertive rather than aggressive
This can be a problem area, because many people do not
consider their rights, but tend to put themselves down and

think that they do not have any. The trouble is that asserting rights is increasingly difficult when there are a large number of unemployed and threats of redundancy are rife. It is difficult to be assertive in the workplace when the result may be dismissal. All the same, being assertive is better than being aggressive. Aggression is often the result of hidden or uncontrolled anger and may be directed against the wrong person; it is liable to be much more physical than assertiveness, which means sticking to your beliefs and rights *without* being aggressive. But what are your rights? Here is a list of rights that we can all lay claim to, whether at work or at home:

- You have a right to be angry sometimes.
- You have a right to be wrong sometimes.
- You have a right to make mistakes sometimes.
- You have a right to put yourself first sometimes.
- You have a right to be respected and acknowledged sometimes.

Many people have a low self-image and self-esteem, and their responses sometimes result in either aggressive behaviour or withdrawal. It is difficult to stand up for yourself and your rights if you do not believe that you have any, or if you have done something wrong or something of which you are ashamed. However, even then you have a right to be treated as a human being and respected for what you are.

4   Consider using previous coping strategies
Try to remember how you coped with similar situations in the past. What can you learn from remembering this? Did previous strategies work, and if not why not? Try to adjust your strategies accordingly. If they didn't work, try something else.

5   Rehearse what you want to say or do
If you feel that you have to face somebody and tell him or her what you think or feel, go through in your mind what

you want to say or do and rehearse it well—perhaps in front of a mirror. Write it down, make it quite clear, and be prepared to stick to your agenda. Also, be ready for others to be surprised at your behaviour. You might also rehearse it with a partner or friend in a role-play.

6   Be realistic
Do not have unrealistic expectations of yourself, of others or of the outcome. Face up to the reality of your situation. If you have made a mistake, admit it and, if appropriate, apologise. If you have been wronged or mistreated, seek help from someone appropriate such as a union representative or welfare officer.

7   Be prepared to accept or to change
Look at the possibility of accepting things as they are—this is also being realistic. Some things we cannot change and some things we can shift just a little. If you cannot change it you may have to learn to live with it and adjust accordingly. If you are able to change things, then do so. Perhaps you can change your job or position or the situation? You may also be able to change your attitude. A small shift or change in one area can be quite significant in affecting other areas of life.

8   Be outgoing
Try to find new interests or revive old hobbies. Join a club or group. Build on what you already can do and have. Try to ensure that your work or the causes of the stress are not the centre of your life and thoughts. Take up some form of physical activity or recreation.

9   Examine your beliefs
Take a close look at your attitudes and beliefs in all areas of your life. Do you have any religious faith that may help? Do you have any positive beliefs about your life, about purpose and meaning? If you do, what are they and how do they

affect and influence you? Do they hinder you in any way,
and can you adjust or change them?

10 *Try to relax*
Learn relaxation techniques. Have massages or learn to
meditate or pray—if this is appropriate. There are a number
of relaxation tapes on the market, mostly based on controlling breathing while lying down, and tightening and then
relaxing different parts of the body in turn. Listening to
your favourite music can also help, especially while lying
down or sitting with a personal stereo.

11 *Take a break*
If possible, take a break from your present work or lifestyle.
Go on holiday or find somewhere you can just be quiet—in a
garden, park or church or out in the countryside. Walking,
cycling and swimming can all help. Buy some new clothes,
if you can afford to. Go parachuting or hang-gliding, or learn
something new to you such as sailing or rock-climbing, or go
on a course at your local college or school.

12 *Use laughter and your sense of absurdity*
It may seem difficult—or even impossible—but *try* to find
something humorous in the situation. If a person is the
cause, imagine him or her in a ridiculous or vulnerable
posture—wearing a silly hat, asleep, having sex or not
wearing any clothes. Also, think of your own part in this
and see if there are any absurdities in what you have said or
done, or in the way you reacted or are reacting.

13 *Seek help*
Consider going to talk to a doctor, welfare officer, occupational health nurse, counsellor, minister or priest, therapist
or someone from an organisation relevant to your problems.
It can help just to talk to someone (as this book aims to
demonstrate). It is not a sign of weakness to ask for
help—indeed, it sometimes takes courage to do so.

COPING WITH STRESS AT WORK

There are specific ways in which stress levels can be prevented from rising, or reduced:

1   *Get your priorities right*

- What is important in your work?
- What are and are not your responsibilities?
- Do not try to be all things to all people.
- Accept that you do and will make mistakes.
- Look at your responsibilities outside work. How important is what you are doing at work compared with your family, partner, children or home?
- Do not take on more than your fair share of the workload.
- Place your tasks in order of importance and priority and tackle them in that order.
- Do not try to do more than one thing at a time, but concentrate on the task in hand.

2   *Manage your time*
This flows from point 1 above:

- Decide how much time you can allocate to each task, and do not give more time to a job than it either needs or deserves.
- Some tasks should be given limited time, as they can be very demanding and draining physically and mentally. If you are in the listening role, for instance, have more and shorter appointments rather than fewer and longer ones. Make time for yourself. If it helps, instead of getting out of bed at the last minute and rushing everything, get up half an hour earlier and take time just to sit and relax or read or listen to the radio.
- Make time for family, hobbies, outside interests and friends.

3   Learn to say 'No'

- Learn to say 'No' when you need to. Many people have difficulty in doing so, and take on more than they can reasonably manage. This raises stress levels. Say 'No' firmly, politely and calmly and make sure that you stick with this decision—'It's very good of you to ask me and to think of me, but I'd rather not, thank you.'

4   Share and delegate

- Do not try to do everything yourself or imagine that you are the only one who can do it—'The graveyard is full of indispensable people'.
- Learn to trust others, where you can, and give them tasks. This assumes that you have good communication with your colleagues and know who can do what. If you feel that there is room for improvement in this area, get to know what their capabilities are and learn to refer work to them.
- Give responsibility to juniors or new people, for they need to learn, even if they make mistakes.
- Beware of being isolated or of isolating yourself. This can result in the attitude that says, 'I'm the only one who can do this and nobody cares about me. I'm the only one who does any work around here.'

5   Seek and expect support

- Seek support, and expect it, from colleagues and others. Arrange to discuss your work with them, and talk to them just to get to know them and to enjoy their company. If you are supervised, get to know your supervisor and let him or her get to know you.
- Keep in touch with your superiors regularly and let them know that you are there—without annoying or pestering them or giving them the impression that you are 'creeping'. This reminds them not only of your presence but of their responsibility for you and for your well-being.

6   *Take time off*

It is essential to have breaks from the routine of work:

- Always have a mid-morning tea or coffee break and a break for lunch. Do not get into the *habit* of snatching a sandwich while working at your desk or bench. Working lunches may be usual practice in some set-ups, but don't resort to them too often.
- Try to have set work hours and a routine. It can sometimes help to have an impromptu break in your routine, but it's usually better to know when you are going to start and finish work. This can vary, of course, especially when you have an important task to do and you work extra time in order to finish it; at the end, you feel a sense of achievement. Keep a balance between having a routine and making changes.
- If you have to take work home, tackle it in the same manner as you would at work, and work out a strategy and routine. Try not to 'dabble' in your work every few minutes or so, because this means that you will keep switching on and off.
- When you are away from work, treat the telephone or requests for help from work with respect. But, if you can, do not let them distract you from your break. It is too easy to say, 'Well, I decided to do it because I wasn't doing anything anyway.'
- Have an outside interest that is not connected with work.

7   *Take regular exercise, meals and sleep*

- Get into the habit of doing some kind of exercise, even if it is only going for a walk in the evening or at the weekend. Swimming is a good all-round way of exercising. Eat regularly and healthily, and once in a while go out for a meal, for a change. Try not to eat a large meal just before you go to bed.
- Try to go to bed at the same time each evening, and establish a routine.

- Get up each morning at the same time—although you may have a lie-in occasionally as a treat.

8 *Go on courses and workshops*

- Go on courses or workshops—workplaces sometimes offer these for members of staff (often paid for by the firm). They keep your mind active and alert as well as up-to-date. Also, you will encounter new people and new ideas and techniques.
- Go on courses that have nothing to do with your work. These can bring fresh stimulation as well as relaxation and, possibly, new interests and people.

These are all suggestions for coping with the stresses of life, especially of work. The trouble is that once an individual's stress level rises above a certain point, he or she will usually find it more and more difficult to use them and to acknowledge that there is a problem. Denial can be quite a powerful reaction to stress.

Being offered such a list of strategies for coping can, for a depressed person, be rather like being told, 'Pull yourself together', when that is precisely what he or she cannot do. So these suggestions are useful as preventive measures, but the stress level will need to be constantly monitored so that the strategies may indeed be put into practice. Remember that they may work when stress levels *begin* to rise, but may not be of much use for someone who is in real distress or on the verge of a breakdown.

All managers, supervisors and other members of staff need to be aware of the causes and effects of stress, whether it results from personal or personality factors, or from stressors and stresses at home or work. As mentioned earlier, stress can also be caused by any combination of these, and can manifest itself in any one or all three areas. The listening helper should be aware of this and be able to direct people to those who can best help—probably via the occupational health unit or welfare officer. Where the stress comes from outside the workplace, such as a difficult marriage or problems with children, relevant outside organisations may need to be consulted (see pages 256–7).

EFFECTS OF CHANGE AND STRESS ON CHILDREN

It is important to know something of how stress can affect children, for a person at work who is suffering from stress may be extra-anxious because of the reactions of her children. Listeners may have to explain this to clients.

1   Play
Children often find it difficult to express feelings verbally, sometimes because they do not have the vocabulary. Instead, they may act out their feelings through what they do and in how they behave rather than in what they say. Some may become aggressive in their play or in their relationships at home or school, or show anger and aggression towards their parents or siblings. Others may retreat into silence and live in their own enclosed world, either by staying at home, perhaps in their bedroom, or by remaining solitary and alone when outside. They may also show feelings through the way they play and the games they develop. Play that incorporates violence or angry or authoritative figures are common, such as games about war and destruction, accidents or disasters:

> A little boy played with Lego when his father, a soldier, was away in the Gulf War, often used Lego men in games where there were car accidents and the men were hurt and had to be bandaged.

Drawings can also express what a child is feeling or thinking—some counsellors or psychologists are experts in art therapy.

2 Feelings

Children may express some of the emotions shown by adults:

- Fear is common, and children can be afraid of any changes that take place in their lives or in the lives of those around them. There may be new homes, schools, environment and friends to be coped with. This fear may cause excitement, hyperactivity and anxiety, or a retreat into isolation, inactivity and silence.
- Blame and guilt can be assumed and felt by children, even when it is not their fault. They may blame themselves for parents being under stress in their everyday lives, in their marriages and relationships, or at work. They may also blame themselves and feel guilty about parents arguing, separating or divorcing. In cases of child abuse, it is common for children to blame themselves rather than the abuser.
- Anxiety may be shown through extra sensitivity to criticism, or to being punished physically or verbally.
- Non-specific or specific illnesses can result. There can be headaches and tummy-aches, listlessness and a general feeling of tiredness and of being unwell.

It can help if children are told what the stresses or problems are, and if they are not kept in the dark by parents on the assumption that:

'We mustn't upset the children—they are too little to understand, so don't tell them.'

This will only cause more distress and anxiety, for the children will feel and experience stress from the changes taking place in their parents. This will rub off into their lives generally. They may need more hugs and cuddles than usual, although some, to the consternation of parents, may reject their affection in an attempt to punish parents for what is happening and for what they don't understand.

3   Redundancy

Redundancy is a problem feared and faced by many people, and it creates in addition a number of other problems. We live in a society where it is still expected that most people above a certain age should work, until retirement. We go to school and then move into a job, or we go from school to college or university and then into a job or profession. The protestant work ethic that we have inherited from previous generations tells us that everyone has to earn his or her place in society through work, and that all able-bodied people should contribute to the welfare both of themselves and of those less fortunate. As well as an income, work gives a person dignity and status in the community.

At least, that is the idea. But this is far from reality for many people, and the number of unemployed in our society runs into millions. Some have left school and through no fault of their own have never worked because they have been unable to get a job. It has been said that there are people leaving school now who may never work. Government policy has been to keep some people unemployed for political and economic reasons. One government minister said that it was worth having some people unemployed in order for economic recovery to take place—it is doubtful whether those who were unemployed at the time would have agreed with him. Many who are made redundant join the ranks of the unemployed and become 'job seekers' in a market where there may be few, if any, jobs available. To be made redundant or to be unemployed is, for most people, a disaster that affects both their personal and their social lives. It can cause ill health, marital and relationship problems, financial distress and feelings of rejection, and result in low self-esteem and the destruction of their sense of purpose in life.

Given such an economic climate, it is necessary for supervisors and managers to understand what problems are created by redundancy, how it may affect both those who are made redundant and those around them. Decisions may be made by management, for whatever reasons, to make certain people redundant, and those who have to tell them the bad news or cope with them in the workplace until they leave need to bear a number of factors in mind.

Perhaps the first is that the threat of redundancy alone can be enough to cause problems for those in work, and jealousy and anxiety about other people can easily arise. 'Watching your back' is a common reaction, the fear being that others may try to ensure that it is you who are first in line for dismissal. It can also result in a lack of trust and, in the case of a team or group, a lack of solidarity and team spirit.

However, the main effect will be a sense of loss, for the experience of being made redundant is one of losing not just a job, but of what this means for the individual and for society in general. There is almost always a reduction in income, but there is also a loss of status, of self-esteem and of stability.

EFFECTS OF REDUNDANCY ON THE VICTIM

1 Loss of Status
When we meet someone for the first time, the first thing we ask is often, 'What is your name and what do you do?' What you 'do', which means your work, tells us not only *who* you are, but also *what* you are. Sometimes we are impressed when people tell us what they do, for their job gives them a certain status in our eyes and tells us something about their income. To say, 'I am a doctor'—or an airline pilot, brain

surgeon, solicitor or lawyer—in some people's eyes indicates a higher status than saying, 'I am a labourer' (or a shop
assistant or cleaner). In this way people are usually graded
according to the perceived status of their job or profession,
so when the job goes, this status can go too.

> Mary was a teacher in the village school where she had lived
> and taught for twenty years, and she felt respected and
> valued in the community. The local children all knew her and
> talked to her whenever they met, and parents would stop her
> in the street to chat and ask her advice about their children.
> When she was made redundant, she began to think of herself
> as a 'nobody'. She was no longer 'our teacher' or 'Miss
> Jones', but just another unemployed middle-aged spinster.
> People expressed their sympathy to her, but through losing
> her job she had lost her status in the community.

2   Loss of income

To be made redundant means for most people that there is a
drop in income. Some are given a 'package' of a gratuity or
pension, or both, and this can make life easier for them, but
some receive nothing other than the need to be supported,
either by their savings or by the state. For a few, redundancy
can bring pay-offs of thousands of pounds or even millions,
in gratuities, share options and pensions. The effect of this
on lower-paid workers who are made redundant can be
anger and resentment and a deep sense of injustice. This can
also happen at lower levels, when staff are paid different
redundancy sums.

The drop in income that redundancy almost always
brings affects every area of life. Some may suffer the threat
or experience of having their homes repossessed, while
others may have to move into a smaller house—if they can
sell the one they already have. They may encounter the
problem called 'negative equity', where the value of their
house drops to below the price that they paid for it, although
they are still paying the mortgage for the property at the
higher value. Children may have to move schools and lose

friends and familiar surroundings, and leave the various youth organisations that they have joined. Partners and families will have to adjust to the many changes that will take place, and there may be fewer or no holidays, birthday or Christmas presents and fewer treats or luxuries. The overall effects on relationships, families, marriages and health can be enormous.

Loss of income will be accompanied by loss of security, and with the sudden absence of a regular salary will come social changes:

> John's life revolved around his work, his new home and his family. He enjoyed his work, and his income was sufficient to keep up a high standard of living for himself, his wife and two teenage children. He would go out two evenings a week to meet friends from work and have a few quiet drinks in their 'local'. About twice a month he would take his wife out for a meal. His children went riding at the stables three miles away. Suddenly, he was made redundant. His life and the life of his family changed drastically. He could no longer afford to go out with his friends or his wife, and his children had to give up their riding lessons. There were also problems with the mortgage and they had to consider selling their home and moving into a smaller place

The loss of income affects every area of life and, for many, being on the dole or income support feels, and is, demeaning.

3 Loss of self-esteem

Being in work gives a certain meaning and purpose to life. As well as an income, it can provide us with the feeling of being valued by others and the belief that we are serving a useful function. It can give a sense of pride in self and in what we do, but it sometimes does much more than this. For some people, work is not only a job or profession. It becomes an integral part of their personality, character and self-image. It gives them self-esteem and a feeling of worth far beyond just pride or pleasure in *having* a job. This is about 'attachment', which is mentioned in Chapter 4 (on bereavement and loss): some people take their job inside them and internalise it.

The stronger this internalisation and attachment, the stronger will be the effects of redundancy on the personality and the sharper the reduction in self-esteem experienced. Some people are unable to 'let go' of their work and all that it has meant for them, and when they are made redundant they feel deeply that they have lost not just a job, but their purpose in life. Many such people feel a sense of commitment and even of dedication in their work, and to lose all this may be to lose themselves.

For those who do not have this sense of pride in or commitment to a particular job, it may simply be a means of earning money, especially if there has not been any choice or if it is repetitive, boring, dirty or demeaning work. But even they may have a sense of having lost not just a job but something of themselves, especially if they have to go on the dole. Many experience feelings of shame and anger at having to live off the state, and a loss of dignity even when they know that they, like everybody else, have paid their taxes and National Insurance over the years.

4   Loss of stability

The changes taking place in our society mean that for many there is great uncertainty about the future. Even though many do happily change jobs a number of times in their working lives, others feel insecure and threatened and fear that they no longer have the guarantee of working all of their lives, of being in the same job until they retire. Some now work on contract and have a job only for a certain number of months or years, after which they may be dismissed or made redundant and then have to look for work elsewhere. The loss of the certainty of living and working in the same place all your life can create great unease, the feeling that life is no longer stable and secure. Moving house, and leaving families, schools, friends, work colleagues and familiar surroundings may all be factors in this destabilising process.

The losses experienced through being made redundant are similar to those of bereavement, and many of the reactions will be the same as those of grief. Most will cope, but at great expense to their personal and family lives. Some will take the news of redundancy stoically, without apparent reaction and as if accepting it, but this does not mean that they do not feel anything. Others react in a different way:

> One day in a large factory, over thirty people were taken into a room and addressed by a senior manager. He read out a list of names and asked these people to leave the room. There were twelve people left. He then told them that they were being made redundant in two months' time. There was an initial sense of shock, and some were stunned to silence and disbelief. After a short pause, some began to shout angrily and demand to know why this was happening and why to them. What had they done to deserve it, and why them and not those who had been asked to leave the room? One man burst into tears and some pointed out that they had mortgages, and partners, new babies and other children to support. How were they going to cope? When the meeting was over, some stayed together to talk and there was a feeling amongst a few that it didn't really matter anyway. What was the point when they could do nothing? Some made extremely derogatory remarks about the man who had given them the news, about the firm and about their work.

These reactions are typical of loss and grief—shock and denial, anger and depression.

REACTIONS TO REDUNDANCY

1 Shock and denial

After being told about their redundancy, some will carry on and close their eyes, ears and minds to the inevitable. There can be a sense of unreality, a sense that this is not happening and will not happen:

'Surely they can't get rid of me after all these years and after what I have done for the firm? It can't be true.'

Some will be very upset and feel a sense of numbness and look dejected. There can also be resignation:

'I just have to accept it and get on with my life. After all, I can't do anything about it.'

This denial can be powerful to the extent that some may refuse to accept the news and will work and live as though it were not happening.

2   Anger

There may already be anger in the air about changes or redundancies that have taken place previously, and anger is a common and natural reaction:

'Why me and not him or her? What have I done to deserve this? It isn't fair.'

There can be feelings of guilt and self-blame:

'I must have done something wrong.'

Some will feel regret at what they are losing and fear for the future:

'How am I going to cope and manage? What about my wife [husband, partner] and family?'

Anger can be directed at anything and anyone, especially at the person bringing the news, and there may be demands for explanations and reasons. One problem is that sometimes managers and those breaking the news will disclaim any responsibility for the decision, saying that someone higher up made it and that it is for economic, financial or other reasons. This can only make matters worse for all concerned. If possible, the person making the decision should break the news personally, admitting that it is his or her responsibility and then explaining why the decision has been made. This may result in a better understanding, and may be followed by personal interviews and explanations. It will not, however, prevent people from feeling shock and anger. One feeling will be anger at having been rejected:

'I have been pushed aside after all the service and dedication I have given. Why me, and what have I done to deserve it?'

Some may feel a sense of relief that decisions have at last been made and that they now know what is to happen, especially if there have been long delays and uncertainties. This may cause some to switch off from their work and begin to focus their attention elsewhere:

'I have to think of the future, look after myself and my family and find another job.'

So performance may suffer as a result of redundancy news, both before, during and after it happens.

Anger can also be directed at self and at families and colleagues, and this causes problems in relationships both at home and at work. It can also be directed at supervisors and managers, with comments such as:

'It's all right for you. You've still got a job. Don't tell me that I'll soon get another job and that I have to be positive about it. How do you know, anyway, and what do you care?'

Some may become aggressive and unco-operative and feel that nobody cares. This anger may be tinged with and lead on to depression.

3 Depression

Depression can set in at the possibility of redundancy, and some will begin to ask what the point of it all is if this kind of thing is going to happen. To feel that you may no longer be required can be depressing for anyone. To feel that you are no longer wanted results in feelings of rejection, and can lower confidence and self-esteem:

'I must be useless if they get rid of me like this.'

Some may console themselves by thinking or being told:

'Remember, it's not you that is being made redundant. Don't take it personally. It's the job that's going, not you.'

This may be very positive, but it is not how people often feel. The job *may* have gone, but it is human beings and human lives that are being affected. Feelings of utter hope-lessness and helplessness may arise:

'I can do nothing about it. Who is going to help me and my family now? I am just like a cog in a huge impersonal wheel churning away and then being thrown out.'

Loneliness and a sense of isolation are common. Some will feel as if they are being picked on, and will withdraw from colleagues into silence and apathy or feel a burning anger and resentment. They may feel that their work is now without purpose, and may wish to resign and leave immediately rather than suffer the humiliation of working with others who are staying. A lessening of commitment to work and of involve-ment with others may be evident, and the feeling that:

'I'll work from nine until five and not give an ounce more.'

The sense of pointlessness can also lead to a loss of per-sonal identity, so intimately are some people's lives enmeshed with what they do at work. Redundancy can also mean feel-ing a loss of control over one's life—with quite dramatic and traumatic changes in personal, social and family life.

The supervisors and colleagues of those who have been or are about to be made redundant should realise that all of the above reactions are normal. They should not be seen as unusual or as the reactions of moaners or inadequates. Most will cope, in whatever ways, but it may take a great deal of pain and effort for them to do so.

POSSIBLE EFFECTS OF REDUNDANCY ON RELATIONSHIPS AND MARRIAGES

- An inability to discuss things with colleagues or partners; a retreat into isolation and loneliness and the feeling that nobody understands or cares.
- A belief that life is uncertain and therefore friendships and relationships are uncertain.
- Constant worry about security, money and the future.
- An increase in the need to show and receive physical affection and love and a clinging to colleagues, friends and partners; *or* a decrease in the need to show and receive physical affection and love and a rejection of partners, family, colleagues and friends.
- Self-blaming, with feelings of being useless and rejected. This can result in a decrease in interest and output at work, and may be reflected in relationships at home: 'If I am no use at work, perhaps I am no use to my family.' This may result in impotence and other sexual problems.
- Anger and frustration directed at anyone, including managers and supervisors, work colleagues, family and friends.
- Panic and anxiety states with out-of-character behaviour, such as excessive spending or meanness.
- Changes in lifestyle and self-image and a dissatisfaction with and desire to end present relationships.
- More closeness in relationships and a deepening of caring and concern; *or* separation and misunderstanding and a concern or search for independence.

Again, these are normal reactions to either the threat or the actuality of redundancy. But how can listeners and others help?

COPING STRATEGIES

1   Practical help and advice

This should be part of the process and procedure for redundancy—those having to face it should be given help and advice about how it will affect them and what their entitlements are, both financially and practically. Because of the many defences that those who are to lose their jobs will put up and their possible anger, apathy and resentment, managers, supervisors and listeners should offer help proactively:

> Do not wait for people to ask for help and advice, but give it automatically.

If left alone and not offered help, some may sink into despair and become unable to ask for or look for help.

2   Acceptance

To counteract the potential problem of denial, it should be made absolutely clear to the individuals concerned what has happened—that they are being made redundant. Some may not accept it and pretend that it isn't going to happen. But they all need to be made aware of how it will or may affect them and their work, lives, health and families. Personal interviews are important in getting this across and in offering information and advice.

3   Expressing feelings

People should be allowed to express how they feel, no matter what their reactions may be. Let them have a good moan and allow them to express their anger, resentment and bitterness. Supervisors and others should not disclaim responsibility or try to protect the firm or organisation. Some victims of redundancy may react by saying:

> 'Well, never mind. These things happen. I've just got to accept it and get on with it.'

But it is far healthier when emotions are expressed and allowed to emerge. As with the grief of bereavement, the expression of emotions can eventually lead to healing and renewal. The problem with redundancy is that the individual has lost what he has and is, and may never work again. Supervisors and others need to learn not to make unhelpful comments such as:

> 'Don't moan about it. You have to look on the bright side and be positive. You'll soon get another job.'
> 'I don't want to hear your moans, thank you. You've got to accept it and face up to it, and the sooner you do this the better for everyone concerned.'
> 'Stop going on about it. You'll only upset others and lower morale.'

Such remarks are likely to result in even more moaning and anger:

> In one large organisation there was a 'moaning coffee' session organised in a room every day at 11.00 a.m., where those being made redundant could meet to talk and express what was going on in their lives.

4 Acknowledgement by others

Those in positions of authority must acknowledge that it will not be easy for those who have been made redundant to cope. And these people need to know that their reactions and feelings and the likely effects of their redundancy *are* being acknowledged by those responsible for making the decisions. It is also often helpful for managers and supervisors to be seen around the workplace showing concern about what is to happen. They should talk about redundancy with the victims. This doesn't mean that it should be mentioned every time they meet, but neither should those in authority pretend that it isn't happening.

5   Spouses, partners and families

It is easy to forget that those made redundant have lives, commitments and responsibilities outside work. They often have partners and children, as well as mortgages, cars and other things they may have to lose. In some cases, welfare officers or others might be encouraged to visit families and offer them help and advice.

Redundancy brings change and change presents a challenge, but in the present climate, and possibly for some time to come, it promises to bring personal and financial disaster for many. In other words, although there may for some be positive elements in the situation, for most redundancy will bring changes that are almost entirely negative. Some will experience massive upheavals in their lives, and will descend into poverty and apathy. Some may never work again.

It is worth adding that those who face retirement can experience many of the symptoms and reactions of those made redundant.

4 Bereavement and Loss

It is certain that a supervisor, manager or other employee within the work environment will at some time encounter the problem of bereavement. It may be that an individual has to be given the news of a death while she is at work, or that someone is returning to work after a bereavement. What should and should not be said or done, and how is the bereaved likely to react and be affected? It is essential to know this. Such knowledge will help not only the listener and helper, but especially the bereaved person, because appropriate and sensitive responses from others can assist the process of grieving. Equally, the wrong responses can hinder and prolong any movement towards acceptance, healing and renewal.

Death is probably the most taboo subject in society. Like sex and mothers-in-law, both sensitive and sometimes threatening subjects, we tend to make jokes about death, perhaps in the vain hope that it will go away and not come to our door. Woody Allen, the American comedian, when asked if he was afraid of dying, replied, 'I'm not frightened of dying. I just don't want to be there when it happens!' But death is one of the few certainties about life and is an experience that we will all have to face at some time—that of others and, finally, our own.

PROBLEMS TO DO WITH DEATH

Death presents a number of problems in our society, not least the fact that we rarely talk about it and even try to deny its existence. There is often a lack of contact with death, a general reduction in social support, a shortening of rituals and a lack of any firm religious or other beliefs to help us face it.

1 Denial of the reality of death

Trying to deny the existence of death is the first problem. We say that the dead person is 'sleeping', is 'at peace', 'resting', 'with the Lord' or 'gone to heaven', or that he or she has been 'called home'. Some believe that these ways of putting it are accurate enough, but they *can* mean that we are denying the simple fact that someone is dead. This denial, the first defence against facing up to the reality of the presence of death, is partly the result of basic human fear: fear of the unknown, fear of darkness, fear of pain, fear of oblivion, of non-existence. (It may also be tied in with fears of punishment, guilt and failure.) It is certainly the fear of losing someone we love, but it is also our fear of what may happen to us when *we* die, and, for some, the fear of what may happen afterwards. There may also be anxiety about those we leave behind and their ability to manage without us. Some will stress the actual fear of dying and the possible pain associated with it:

'I wouldn't like to linger on in severe pain, but would rather die suddenly in my bed.'

Whatever the reasons, the denial of the reality of death means that it is not usually faced as a hard fact and a present reality, and we exclude it from our thoughts and conversation. As well as being our way of coping with the fear of death and of dying, denial is also usually one of the first reactions to being bereaved.

2 Lack of contact with death

We live in a world where people are generally healthier than ever before. We are constantly told by the media that to be young is everything and to be old is to be ugly and undesirable. We also speak of 'senior citizens' rather than old people, as though being old were an embarrassment. Although people often live to a ripe old age, it is possible that our society is becoming more and more clinical about dying. That death is seen by many as something to be hidden away is demonstrated by the fact that usually the dead are removed from our presence as soon as possible, sometimes in the mistaken belief that this will help to avoid some of the pain of loss and make it easier for us to cope. It may also be that hiding the dead away in this manner is an attempt by others to avoid the responsibility of having to cope with our grief. At one time the dead were kept at home, and some will still remember seeing a loved one or friend 'laid out' in the front room or local church.

Also, families are more dispersed than ever before. Often parents, children and other relatives are scattered not only throughout the country, but over the world. Even though there are something approaching one million single-parent families in the United Kingdom and the 'nuclear family' comprising parents plus children is no longer the norm in our society, in some ways the nuclear family has become more important than the extended family. All this means that extended-family bonds may be looser than in previous generations, so that when someone dies there is less chance of others being in contact, except perhaps for the funeral.

Many people die in hospital or hospices rather than with their families and friends. This may be beneficial for the person dying in terms of medical care and attention, but it does mean that people sometimes die away from those they love. So death is no longer a part of many people's experience of life.

3   Diminished social support

In the days when death involved not only the family but the whole community, people would turn out for a funeral and line the streets. Rarely now do we see people stop or men raise their hats when a cortège passes by. The 'wake', though, is still observed in some parts of the country: here the dead person lies in an open coffin in the house while the family and friends gather to pay their respects. In this way the sadness of the loss is expressed, and the life of the deceased person celebrated.

Often, death causes great embarrassment, not only to the bereaved who may be made to feel like social outcasts, but also to friends and neighbours. Sometimes people will cross the road to avoid meeting the bereaved and, perhaps worst of all, if they do meet them they never mention the one who has died. After a few weeks, it is often expected that everyone and everything will be back to normal, and some will even say:

'I don't want to hear about it. It's morbid. Anyway, it's three months so you should be over it by now.'

Generally we seem to lack the solidarity of the support and understanding of the wider community to help us to face bereavement.

4   *Absence of rituals*
This is not so much an absence of any rituals at all after a death, but the tendency to reduce the extent of the funeral and accompanying rituals and a shortening of any period of mourning. The view often is:

'Let's get it over with and return to normal as quickly as we can.'

In dealing with stillborn babies, until recently there was little or no contact with the dead child; parents were simply told to wait and try again later and the body was disposed of without any rituals whatsoever. It has now been realised that there is a need to mark a stillbirth by allowing the parents to hold the baby and to have a funeral. Rituals such as memorial or thanksgiving services and funerals help people to realise that the person is dead and can help them to face the loss, as well as giving dignity to the person who has died and providing an opportunity for relatives and friends to mourn and to begin, or continue, the process of grieving. And viewing the body may help some people to face the reality of the death.

5 Loss of belief

The decline in orthodox religious beliefs may mean that some people, with little or no faith to sustain them, find it more difficult to face and live with bereavement and death. A strong belief in heaven, in reincarnation, in life after death, or the humanistic belief that we should give thanks for a person's life, can all help people to accept a death. They do not necessarily make the loss any easier, but they can help. In the absence of such beliefs, the process of grieving becomes more and more difficult. The disappearance or diminution of many of the internal as well as external supports presents problems for those who attempt to help the bereaved, whether as family, friends, colleagues, listeners or counsellors. We need to accept death as a fact and as part of the normal process of life.

HELPING THE BEREAVED

As mentioned earlier, most people do not know what to say when they meet someone who has been bereaved, and this may explain why so many avoid mentioning the event. But to ignore a bereavement is an insult both to the living and to the dead and will almost certainly be taken as such:

> 'I met her and she didn't even mention my husband. It's as though he never existed.'

More than anything else, the bereaved usually have a desire to talk about their loved one, and they should be encouraged to do so. So never avoid mentioning the person who has died, and at the simplest level say:

> 'I am sorry to hear about the death of your husband [mother, child, brother]. It must be awful for you.'

Even the plainest words of sympathy will help. Pretending that the death has not happened or believing that it will soon be out of mind will only compound the problem. Not that it is usually easy to know what to say—and if you are not sure, then don't say anything except that you are sorry. If the relationship permits it, you could touch the bereaved person's arm or give him or her a hug. Simply being there and sharing his or her grief is not only the least we can do, it is sometimes the best. But don't run around trying to do everything for the bereaved. They are not ill, and often feel a strong need to do things for themselves. Nothing can help more than letting them know that you care and are available should they need to talk.

The problem is that although the dead person has gone, he is still there and will not go away. People never 'get over' a death, for the experience has happened to them and will remain part of their life. They can try to push it aside and ignore it, but it remains a fact. It is an experience we need to go through, and if we face up to it we will gradually learn to live with it.

It is sometimes assumed that if a child dies and there are other children in the family, then it helps to remind people that they should be thankful for their other children.

'Matthew has died, but you should be grateful that you have two others.'

This is not true, for nothing and nobody can take the place of someone who has died. The fact that there are other children is meaningless, for one has gone. A parent may indeed feel that his other children help him to cope because they have to be cared for, but he does not see them as replacements for the one who has died. Similarly it is sometimes thought that a new baby can be a suitable replacement. This is also usually not true. In one case of the death of a twin, neighbours thought that the mother should be grateful because she had one baby left. In fact, the mother was torn between the joy of having a baby and the sorrow at one having died. She was experiencing the two emotions simultaneously.

The same applies to adult deaths. The fact that the person who has died was older does not make the death easier to accept. People will say, 'He had a good innings', and this may be true, but the death is still a tragedy for those who love him or her. They are no less bereaved and still need to grieve.

THE GRIEVING PROCESS

In order to understand grief it is necessary to understand the experience of loss generally. I regularly mislay my car keys and know how I react when I do. I am annoyed that it has happened and can't believe that I have lost them yet again. They must be somewhere and it must be somebody else's fault. Who can I blame? I am angry at not being able to remember when I last had them and frustrated at the sheer inconvenience caused. I riffle through my pockets and briefcase over and over again and search high and low throughout the house. Tied in with all this is the anxiety that I will be late for my next appointment. After a while I may begin to feel that it doesn't matter anyway, and the anger begins to turn into apathy. When I do eventually find them I experience a great sense of relief, although I may still be annoyed that it has happened. This is only one of life's minor inconveniences, but if I can feel such varied and strong emotions over the loss of a set of keys, how much more will I feel when I lose someone I love?

Loss is a normal human event and we all experience it from birth throughout our lives. We attach ourselves to objects and people around us and they become vital parts of our lives. The attachment can be even stronger than this, in that they become part of who and what we are. We take them into ourselves and identify ourselves with them, and them with us. In fact, it is only when we first relate to other people and the world around us that we become individuals, and it is this that enables us to develop a sense of worth and self-identity. But if we attach ourselves to objects and people we are likely to lose them, and then we will feel the pain of loss and separation. Also to love entails laying ourselves open to the possibility of loss and pain. When associated with bereavement, this pain is called grief. Unlike physical pain it cannot usually be treated with drugs, and in order for us to cope and for healing to begin it must be allowed to happen to us. To cover it over and pretend that it isn't there, or to try to keep a 'stiff upper lip' or see it as something to be 'got over', will only result in further or prolonged suffering.

As a process, grief affects people in certain common ways, which can be outlined into four main stages—not separate stages but possible reactions within a wide spectrum of emotions and physical sensations. Some people never experience some of the reactions, while others may move progressively through the stages. For one person, one set of reactions and feelings may be long and drawn out, while for another they may be brief or non-existent. At one moment they are in shock and the next they are depressed. This can be followed by bouts of anger and a return to denial, with a period of calm and numbness. At another time the feelings and reactions are all mixed up together.

It is unhelpful to see these stages as representing a certain time frame. It is sometimes said that shock and denial can last about six months, anger another six months or so, then depression about a year; finally, after a total of two years or so, healing takes place and the bereaved begin to learn to live again. This may be true in specific cases, but it does not represent reality for most people. Although it is true that it takes at least two years for most to begin to progress to any kind of healing, the process of grieving takes a lifetime and people learn to live with it. When dealing with someone who has been bereaved, think of two years as the minimum period rather than, as is more popularly held, a few months, after which everything is supposed to be over and dealt with. One simple way of remembering the first three stages and the process is via the word SAD—shock, anger and depression.

Stage 1: Shock
The first reaction to the news of a death is usually one of shock. This can bring with it anything from feelings of numbness and emptiness to hysteria and collapse. Usually there are so many things to be done after a death that the numbness and denial actually enable the bereaved to cope and carry on with the preparations for the funeral and the legal and practical matters that arise. Often there are sensations of coldness, fainting or weakness. Crying is also common. However, shock can be delayed and experienced much later:

> One woman whose husband died displayed no feelings whatsoever other than a coldness and sense of isolation. This went on throughout the funeral and afterwards, but when the dog was killed three months later she broke down and began to grieve uncontrollably. Neighbours said that she cared more for the dog than she had for her husband. They were wrong, and what she was manifesting was delayed grief. The death of the dog broke her last reserves and her grief came pouring out.

There can also be strong feelings of unreality.

'It hasn't really happened.' 'It can't happen to me.' 'He can't be dead. I saw him just this morning before I came to work.'

People may refuse to accept the news for a considerable time:

'He'll walk through the door at any minute. I can hear his footsteps outside.'

Some will even say that they experience the presence of their loved one with them:

'I can still feel him around me. His pipe is on the table and his clothes are in the wardrobe.'

This sense of shock, unreality and denial are normal reactions, and those who experience them should be reassured that they are not going mad, as some occasionally believe.

So the main reaction at this stage is usually:

'It hasn't happened.'

Stage 2: Anger

Anger is sometimes difficult to accept because it seems destructive. However, it can be one way in which to try to retain or recover some kind of control in a situation where we may seem to have no control at all. Anger in bereavement can lead to the need to find someone to blame. And it can be directed at anyone and everyone, especially at the dead person who has been so inconsiderate as to die:

'How could she show such lack of care as to die at such an inconvenient time?'

She must have died for a reason, and it must be someone's fault. It might be the doctor—'He should have been able to save him'; or God—'How can a loving God allow such a thing to happen?' The anger may also be directed at the person bringing the bad news. Even the sight of people laughing, loving or just being alive can cause outbursts of anger and grief. The bereaved person may, for instance, on returning to work become angry and upset because others are getting on with their lives:

'How can they behave like this when they don't know how it feels?'

There can also be strong feelings of guilt and self-blame:

'It's my fault. I shouldn't have had that argument with her last night. I wasn't even able to say goodbye or that I loved her.'

Tied in with these feelings of anger and guilt is anxiety:

> 'What am I going to do without her? How will I live? Should I sell the house and move, or should I stay where I am with all the memories around me? What about the funeral? How will I cope with it all?'

Longing and searching for the loved one are also common reactions. Longing can be described as a deep ache, an excruciating inner pain, which needs the presence of the loved one. There can be a crying out for the one who has gone and feelings of immense sadness:

> 'I want him here to share my life. Why isn't he with me now—I need him so much?'

Searching may take the form of roaming the streets looking for the person who has died and expecting to see him at any moment. Some even think they see their loved one in crowds, in the street, on a bus or train or in a shopping centre. This searching is a natural response to the separation and the fact that the loved one has gone—and if he has gone, then he must be somewhere! Some may find solace in religious beliefs or in spiritualism, for instance; or go over memories of the past and try to relive previous experiences. Some will feel a strong need to get rid of all the clothes and other belongings of the dead person and give them to the Salvation Army or some other organisation. Others, though, will wish to keep certain items as special reminders. And in some cases everything belonging to the dead person will be kept and treasured, and his room may even become a shrine to his memory, left just as it was when he died. Restlessness and irrational behaviour are common in the bereaved, sometimes as a result of the search for the one who has gone. The trouble is that there can be no real substitute for the loved one, and nothing can fill the void.

So the main reaction at this stage is usually:

> 'Why me?' 'Why us?' 'Why him?' 'Why her?' 'Why?'

Stage 3: Depression

The experience of depression is common. It can be as though when the initial shock has moved into anger and when no answer comes to the demand to know 'Why?', the bereaved person can only descend into the depths. The result can be a complete lack of interest in anything, an apathy towards life in general. Everything seems to slow down and life may seem meaningless:

> 'What's the point of it all? It's all a waste of time. All we ever lived for has gone, and life makes no sense any more.'

This lack of purpose and meaning can also develop into a loss of self-esteem:

> 'I am nothing any more and I am useless without her.'

Some may seem to be on the verge of a breakdown and may need medical, counselling or psychiatric help if they move into chronic grief. In those who are religious, depression can also bring a loss of all belief, while some may discover a new sense of purpose and a new faith.

One problem presented by our society is that a woman is often labelled according to her husband's job, or status in the community. She has been the 'wife of' rather than an individual in her own right, and may now feel that she has lost her identity and that nobody wants her any more:

> 'When my husband was alive I was invited out, but now nobody wants to know me or cares.'

This loss of identity can also apply to a man, for a man's life may also be intimately linked with that of his partner. The result may be a deep sense of loneliness and isolation. The house seems empty now, and there doesn't seem to be any meaning or purpose in working or living without her. Not being physically loved is also an important factor in the loss, and this too can be hurtful and isolating. It may also happen that other people avoid physical contact with the bereaved person, which only deepens his feelings of loss and rejection.

So the main reaction at this stage is usually:

'Why bother? What's the point and purpose of it all?'

Stage 4: Acceptance and healing

Perhaps the most difficult thing for the bereaved or the helper to understand is that the very pain and loss of grief has within it the seeds of healing and renewal. If we are allowed to grieve and experience the suffering, and to express the many complex emotions that it brings, we will almost certainly move on to acceptance and to the feeling that we can live again. We need to have 'gone through' rather than 'got over' the reactions and emotions. If we are helped to face up to the loss rather than deny it, then we will move forward and feel that life is worth living. If we truly love, then we must grieve, and this grieving must take place within and around us. We will survive whatever happens, but surviving is not the same as living. I may survive an accident but be badly injured, and the damage may be permanent if I am not treated successfully. The treatment for the bereaved person is to let her grieve through a process known as catharsis, in which she is allowed to give vent to her emotions. Moving through the pain means moving on towards healing and renewal.

This does not mean that there will be no more crying, no more tightness in the chest or throat, no more sadness or feelings of anger and depression, but it does mean that life will become more bearable. Part of the process is the slow realisation that things can never be the same again. The dead cannot come back to life as we knew them, but we can believe that they are with us in some new way. This is not a denial or blocking of reality, for we cannot and should not forget the past. Rather, it is a turning towards the realisation of a new sense of well-being and the knowledge that we will and can cope. For some, this is connected with a new sense of identity and a growing sense of the presence of the lost person, especially if that person was a partner or close friend. As time passes, identification with him or her can become stronger. In her book, *Death and the Family*, Lily Pincus says that it was many years after her husband's death that she began to feel a strong sense of his presence, and that this feeling grew even stronger as time passed. This is not necessarily a spiritual or ghostly experience, but the inner knowledge that the other person is still there and has again become part of what makes us who we are. Lily Pincus speaks of this as an 'internalisation' of the person who has died. It is something like making the dead person live again in our minds and memories so that he or she does not fade away or get pushed into the background. This experience is powerfully outlined in the film, *Truly, Madly, Deeply*,[1] where the bereaved woman is only able to move on into a new life and relationship when her dead partner comes back to her again.

There can be many other reactions to bereavement, such as helplessness and sometimes relief, especially when someone has been terminally ill. There can be physical sensations such as sensitivity to noise and to other people, depersonalisation like an 'out of body experience', breathlessness and a dry mouth, and hollowness in the stomach. Confusion and hallucinations, sleeplessness, loss of memory and appetite, social withdrawal, dreams and nightmares, avoiding anything likely to bring back memories—all these and more may be experienced by the bereaved.

HOW CAN YOU, THE LISTENER, HELP?

- Do not ignore the fact of the death, and do use the words 'died' and 'dead' rather than 'passed on' or 'gone to

---

[1] Available on video—and recommended to anyone who is grieving, or who wants to understand grief.

sleep'. This is to help the bereaved person to realise what has happened and to break through a possible defence of denial and unbelief.

- Say you are sorry about what has happened, and ask if you can do anything to help. This might elicit the response, 'Yes. Bring my wife back', but you make the offer saying at the same time that you are around if he wishes to talk or if there is anything at all that you can do. Even if bereavement has happened to you, never say:

'I know how you feel.'

Different people grieve in different ways, even in the same family or group, and nobody can ever know exactly how someone else feels. You can only know how you feel.

- Do talk about the dead person, or, if you never knew her, encourage the bereaved person to talk about her. If it is a baby that has died, the mother might speak about her dashed hopes for the future and about what she had expected.
- Ask to see photographs, especially if you did not know the person who has died. This can lead to talking about and remembering past incidents. Some may not wish to look at photographs, finding them too painful at this stage, but if the bereaved person seems to want to show them to you they may be useful in making the loved one real again.
- Allow people to express how they feel, if they wish to do so. Do not be afraid if they break down and cry, and do not say such things as:

'Don't upset yourself. He wouldn't have wanted you to cry.'

This will only make them bury the feelings away. Also, stay with a person who cries, if she will allow you to. Say something such as:

'Don't be afraid or ashamed of crying. It's only natural. Let it come out if you wish.'

You may hug her or hold her hand or put an arm on her shoulder, and don't be afraid to cry too. This is perfectly natural and normal.

- Remember that grieving is a lifelong process and that she will not 'get over it' in a few weeks or months. It is common for people to express sympathy for a short time and then to assume that it is over, but it is still appropriate much later to ask her about it and how she is getting on or feeling. And be prepared for her to say, for instance:

'I think of her every day, and it's forty years since she died.'

- Do not automatically run to the doctor for drugs or medication, for these might delay and suppress the natural grieving process. Sometimes the cry for help, whether medical or of any other sort, is more a sign of the distress of others than of those grieving.
- Give any practical help possible—sorting out papers, files and other personal belongings, making telephone calls, looking at insurance and finance—but do not take over responsibility for things. The bereaved need to be involved, even if they don't feel like it. Otherwise they may say later that they regret not having been able or allowed to do things for themselves. You must not do anything to take away their self-esteem or confidence.

Never say:

'Pull yourself together and think of others.'
'I know how you feel.'
'You must keep strong for the children.'
'Don't cry like that. Look ahead and think of the future.'

'You are still young enough to marry again and you'll probably meet someone else.'
'Sorry to hear about your son—or was it your daughter?'
'You have cheered up a lot lately.'
'It takes time, but you'll eventually get over it.'
'Time is a great healer.'

Most of these might be true, but they are not helpful.

Most people never forget the loved one they have lost: the memories and feelings are always there, buried. They may come rushing to the surface, causing distress and anxiety, but the listening helper must see these responses as normal and allow them to emerge and be expressed. This is the way to renewal and a lasting healing.

5 Post-trauma Stress

Post-trauma stress (PTS) is the stress resulting from a traumatic, violent or shocking incident—anything from an apparently minor accident to a major disaster. It can affect not only the immediate victims and their families but also onlookers, witnesses, friends and colleagues. A major accident or incident in a factory or workplace—for instance, an armed robbery in a bank, building society, shop or factory, or other violence against staff—can affect all those around the victim or victims and those who attempt to help. Post-trauma stress can be defined as:

> the development of certain characteristic symptoms following a psychologically distressing event which is outside the range of normal human experience.

Although the incident is usually one not normally experienced by the victim, if he *has* experienced a similar incident previously he will not necessarily be spared the 'characteristic symptoms'. Not all will suffer the symptoms anyway, but what must be stressed is that to be affected in any way at all is normal. So post-trauma stress can also be defined as 'the normal reactions of normal people to abnormal events'.

The external incidents that can trigger such reactions may be anything that involves violence and that can cause shock and fear: a rape, mugging, or robbery; a road traffic accident or air crash; a break-in at home; a difficult and traumatic divorce. Alternatively, it could be a major disaster similar to the sinking of the Zeebrugge ferry, the Bradford football stadium fire or the Hillsborough stadium tragedy, or the King's Cross Tube station fire in London. Such external incidents can affect individuals, who may take their symptoms in to work. The effects may then spread out from the victims to their colleagues and workmates.

PTS may influence an individual's feelings about himself and others and may affect all his relationships. He and his whole family may then be caught up in difficult and distressing changes outside their usual range of experience. This can cause difficulties at work, absenteeism, marital stress and the breakdown of relationships, ill health and, sometimes, the development of deeper and more disturbing symptoms. When these symptoms persist or intensify for more than a month or so, a condition known as post-traumatic stress disorder (PTSD) can emerge. When PTSD develops, victims are often unable to work and may have difficulty in sustaining relationships. At this stage, the services of a specialist counsellor, psychotherapist, psychologist or psychiatrist will usually be needed. Symptoms can lie dormant and emerge weeks, months and even years later, and reactions can vary from mildly disturbing to incapacitating. PTSD is usually seen as the extension of PTS symptoms to a point where people are unable to cope with their lives, although some do manage to carry on in spite of the symptoms.

> Alan had served in the Falklands War, after which he left the Army and worked in a factory in his home town. He coped well and, to begin with, he showed none of the effects of post-trauma stress. However, gradually symptoms began to emerge and he suffered nightmares and flashbacks. Although he did have many of the symptoms of PTSD he was able to carry on with his work, largely because of the support and understanding that he received from his wife, who was a nurse.

Others are less fortunate, and have to leave work and seek treatment.

CHARACTERISTICS OF POST-TRAUMA STRESS

The three main reactions are re-experiencing the feelings associated with the incident, avoiding any reminders and an arousal of the nervous system.

1   Re-experiencing

Someone who has been involved in an incident can feel that it is happening again, and the sensations and emotions induced at the time can emerge and be re-lived and re-experienced later—in what are known as 'flashbacks'. The individual seems to flash back to the event, and the event seems to flash forward into the present. These feelings can be triggered by an obvious external cause or come as out-of-the-blue experiences.

Reactions can be triggered when something in the present reminds the person of the incident. It may be any sensory experience—to do with sights, sounds, smells, tastes or touching. The sight of a similar event on the television or in a video, for example, may resurrect the feelings from the incident. If someone has been in a traffic accident the sound of a police or ambulance siren at some later date may trigger the old symptoms—as may a bang such as a balloon bursting, a voice, a crashing sound, or even just an ominous silence. Certain smells—petrol, rubber, dampness, disinfectant, sweat or food, for instance—can cause similar reactions.

> A young woman cashier who had been involved in an armed robbery in a building society went home and threw away her husband's after-shave. It was the same after-shave used by the robber and reminded her of him every time she went near her husband.

People can be reminded of an incident by the taste of certain foods, or, after a traffic accident, by that of petrol, oil, alcohol or sweat, or simply a dry mouth. Touching such substances as rubber, metal, skin, flesh or water may also cause flashbacks. The feel of a steering wheel (again, after a road accident) or a piece of equipment in a factory where an accident took place, can have the same effect:

> A number of stewards from the *Herald of Free Enterprise* [the ferry that sank in 1987 with substantial loss of life] after the Zeebrugge incident could not take a bath, even though in this situation they were completely in control. The feel of the water was unbearable. Most of the stewards left within a few months, and at least one still hates the smell of the sea and cannot eat fish.

Although they are distressing and disturbing, these reactions are relatively easy to understand because they can be connected with a very definite and concrete trigger. Out-of-the-blue experiences, on the other hand, can be more difficult, for they occur without any apparent trigger. They can happen anywhere—at home, at work, in the street, while shopping or even while relaxing in bed or in the bath. Because they have no apparent cause, they can be extremely frightening and overwhelming:

> An elderly man recently involved in a violent riot went back to his car, intending to drive home. As he sat in the car he began to hear the air raid sirens from the Second World War and the sound of bombs dropping around him. It was half an hour before he could drive home.

> A young man who had been at the wheel when his car was involved in an accident in which his best friend was killed began to see his friend's face when he looked in a mirror.

> A prison officer who had been involved in a riot was out shopping with his wife when he suddenly found himself sitting on the floor in a supermarket. He was engulfed by feelings of confusion, panic and disorientation. The suppressed feelings suddenly came rushing to the surface, for no apparent reason—the trigger could, though, have been the crowds in the supermarket, the noise and the feeling of being enclosed.

2 Avoidance

Those involved in a traumatic incident may seek to avoid anyone and anything that might remind them of the event. This can include a fear of returning to a particular workplace because being there may bring on symptoms such as fear, panic or anxiety. Such diverse phenomena as anniversaries, identification parades, court cases or media attention can cause similar aversion reactions. Individuals may try to avoid certain thoughts, feelings or situations because of the fear of arousal and re-experiencing. Concentration at work or at home may deteriorate, and some may even lose acquired skills or expertise. Feelings of isolation are common:

> 'Nobody understands. You weren't there so you don't know what it's like.'

Some experience sensations of numbness and find it difficult to express emotions—for example, they may be unable to show love or affection particularly to partners, family or friends. Some cannot or will not think of the future, cannot shake off the feeling that the incident is going to happen all over again. In some cases, especially where lives have been threatened, victims may feel that they haven't got long to live. Obviously, such thoughts and feelings can affect everything—work and careers, relationships and marriages.

Re-experiencing and avoidance are two sides of the same coin. We try to avoid reminders by pushing the feelings down inside our minds, but the more we do this the more we are likely to re-experience symptoms. The more we re-experience symptoms, the more we try to avoid them, and again push the feelings down inside to control them. And so the cycle may start again.

3 Arousal

A traumatic incident makes the nervous system increasingly sensitive to external stimuli. The slightest sound may cause an individual to 'jump' nervously. It may bring on an incapacity to accept the everyday happenings of work, home or family life. Friends or colleagues talking and laughing, or children playing, may lead to outbursts of anger or even violence. Similar situations may cause some to isolate themselves from others in an attempt to avoid the situation:

> A soldier from the Falklands War would lock himself in a room for days at a time and then emerge to treat his wife and family like dirt. He could not stand the normal routine, the noise and bustle, of family life.

This increased arousal can result in sleeplessness and hyper-activity or difficulty in concentrating, and some become over-vigilant, expecting something bad to happen at any time and without warning.

These three particular reactions—re-experiencing, avoid-ance and arousal—are not separate: they are interlinked with each other and with a wide number of other possible symptoms. Reminders can cause arousal, which can resur-rect symptoms and cause re-experiencing, which can lead to attempts to avoid reminders, which can then lead to arousal—and so on in a circle of reactions.

Other symptoms
Denial, as in bereavement, can be very strong in PTS, especially in men, and may prevent people from acknow-ledging that there is a problem or from asking for help. To ask a person how he is after an incident may elicit the reply:

> 'I'm all right, thank you. I don't need any help. I can cope.'

The desire to preserve the 'macho' image, common in men and especially in uniformed organisations or all-male groups, can reinforce this denial. This image is an important coping mechanism, but it does not mean that no feelings are being experienced. What it can mean is that the emotions are hidden away and may emerge later in other ways.

The reactions to traumatic incidents are similar to those of bereavement and loss: any of the following feelings, behaviour and physical effects may occur.

Possible feelings

- A sense of pointlessness—'Why bother? Why carry on?'
- An increase in the level of anxiety and a sense of vulnerability—'It can happen again, and probably will.'
- Sadness and depression.
- Intrusive thoughts and images invading the mind.
- Shame, anger, regret, guilt and bitterness—even when there are no logical reasons for these feelings. A person who rescues others may feel guilty because she was unable to save everybody.
- Survivor guilt—feeling guilty at having survived when others have been injured or have died.
- A sense of isolation and loneliness, *or* strong feelings of solidarity and identity with other victims and survivors.
- Fear of closed or open spaces, and fear of crowds or groups of people.
- Fear of being in the same position or situation again.
- Feeling helpless and useless—that control has been taken away from your life.

Possible behaviour

- An inability to concentrate or make even simple decisions.
- Impulsive actions such as excessive spending or buying things without a reason, the desire to change jobs or move home, changing a lifestyle, or ending or creating new relationships.
- Irritability, anger and, sometimes, violence without any apparent reason.

- Excitement, hyperactivity and agitation.
- Inability to sleep; sleep disturbances, dreams and nightmares.
- Incessantly talking about an incident, *or* refusing to talk about it at all.

Possible physical effects

- Non-specific illnesses—headaches, stomach pains, tightness in the chest, thinking a heart attack is about to take place, generally feeling unwell and being constantly tired.
- An increased sensitivity to noise of any kind, or being especially sensitive about colleagues at work or family at home.
- An increase in smoking or in alcohol consumption; or the desire to get drugs from the doctor such as anti-depressants, tranquillisers or sleeping tablets.

There may be marked changes in values or beliefs or in the way people view themselves. There may be either a decrease or an increase in self-esteem and confidence. A person suffering from PTS may wish to change friendships, jobs or relationships:

> A man in his early fifties was involved in a traffic accident and within a short time had left his wife and family for a woman twenty years younger. He bought himself a sports car and created a new image for himself with new clothes and hairstyle. This is sometimes called the 'middle-aged-medallion-man syndrome'!

He may have said to himself:

> 'What's the point of working or being married and having children or a home if these things can happen? I must look for something new.'

The loss of personal belongings, or when a place of work such as a factory or coalmine is closed down or a home is destroyed, can have similar effects.

WHY DO THESE CHANGES OCCUR?

There are a number of possible explanations. One is based on the life beliefs that most people have grown to accept over the course of their lives. These are (1) a sense of invulnerability; (2) the belief that life has a meaning and purpose; (3) a sense of their own self-esteem.

1   Invulnerability

This is our basic belief—that life is fairly safe and that 'bad things only happen to other people and not to me or us'. Most people do not experience devastating incidents in their lives, and so they tend to grow up believing in their own invincibility. In reality, anyone may experience a heart attack, a car accident or some other tragic event, and we all *know* that bad things can happen, but we could not live our lives fully if we were constantly thinking along these lines. So we push such thoughts to the back of our minds and just get on with living. When something bad does happen, we suddenly know that we are vulnerable—even, in some cases, that we may die or could have been killed. Traumatic incidents challenge our basic belief in our invulnerability; our lives are threatened and our world is turned upside down. We experience fear and may question our very existence.

2   The meaning and purpose of life

Most people believe that life has a meaning and purpose, even if they cannot say exactly what it is. They may not be able to write an essay about it, but would probably say that they find meaning and purpose in loving and living, in their families and friends, perhaps in their work, in their homes and gardens, in possessions and pets, in holidays and hobbies. A traumatic incident can severely call this belief into question, so that a person may say:

> 'If these things can happen, then there is no God, no meaning and no purpose in life.'

If you are involved in an accident or if someone you love is killed or dies, if your life is threatened or in danger, then life can seem to be without purpose and point.

3 Self-esteem
Most of us tend to believe: 'I am not a bad person.' At least, we are as good or as bad as anyone else! We hope that if something problematical happened we would 'do the right thing', whatever that might be. However, when something traumatic happens, this feeling of self-esteem, or self-respect, may be challenged:

> Following a tragic accident at work, Graham believed that he could have done something to prevent it, and blamed himself—'I should have been able to do something to help and protect people.' He was a body-building expert and thought that because of this he should have prevented the accident from happening. He was not responsible, but he still felt that he had failed both other people and himself.

It is common for men to feel guilty because they have not protected women, and for parents to believe that they should have protected children.

The symptoms of PTS are partly the result of this attack on and disturbance of our personal values and beliefs. We realise that we are breakable and can die, we question the meaning and purpose of life, and we can lose our self-esteem or find it diminished.

The suppression of emotions
It can also be argued that the symptoms arise because we try to suppress our emotions. We bury the fear and horror, the sights we have seen, the sounds we have heard—the whole experience—deep within our minds, and we cover them over with what we think are hard shells. Unfortunately, these shells have a habit of breaking or opening up when we least expect them to, so that the experiences, the sensations

and emotions that they hide come bursting up through the surface. (Also, they can be triggered by external reminders.) This suppression takes a great deal of emotional and mental energy that we cannot sustain all of the time. We may pretend that we are not affected, but something may happen to make the sensations come flooding to the surface to disturb or disrupt our lives.

Those who have taken on helping and caring roles during and following an incident can also suffer the symptoms of PTS. So they too may need to talk to someone, especially when the experience is distressing.

TYPICAL EFFECTS OF AN INDIVIDUAL'S PTS ON OTHERS

- When changes take place in the way people see themselves, their work, partner, children and friends, relationships can become strained, showing an inability to communicate.
- If, rather than remaining silent about the incident, the victim can't stop talking about it, others—whether workmates, colleagues, family or friends—may well find it boring, irritating and frustrating.
- When the troubled person has nightmares, perhaps waking up shouting and sweating and in a state of panic, partners may become exasperated—'Not that same old thing again! Why can't you just put it behind you and forget it? I'm sick of being woken up like this.'
- The troubled person's feelings of apathy, that life and work are a waste of time, can infuriate others.
- An inability to make decisions will affect people at work as well as at home—another cause of anger or impatience in colleagues and others.
- When feelings of vulnerability or anxiety are expressed it is easy for others to become unsympathetic—'Pull yourself together and stop going on about it. It's over now.'

- The feelings of everyone involved, including workmates and partners, can be pent up—then suddenly burst out in bouts of anger and shouting.
- Attempts to change work or lifestyle, perhaps by rejecting family or friends, may lead to lack of understanding and even threats of dismissal from work.
- The not uncommon symptoms of a childlike need for affection or understanding, and a clinging to others, can be suffocating for all involved.
- The troubled person may be unsympathetic to the concerns and worries of other people, perhaps trivialising them.
- Expressions of low self-esteem, of shame, fear, guilt and failure, constantly expressed, may exasperate others, provoking them into such comments as 'Well—maybe you are just a wet and feeble person.'

During and immediately following an incident

At the time of a traumatic incident at work, those directly involved need support and help from the people closest to them, especially from colleagues and supervisors. Senior managers should also be present to offer sympathy and to show that they care. Victims may ask for their families, and it is usual to inform families of accidents and other non-minor incidents. The first priority must be to save lives and to get medical help as soon as possible. Victims may need to talk, especially to colleagues and to onlookers or witnesses. At this early stage they do not need counselling. Going through a practical debriefing, sometimes called an 'operational debriefing' by organisations such as the police and armed services, can help. This is when everyone gathers round with a senior person simply to talk through the incident and to check what happened and what people did and why. At this point many will be in a state of shock, whether mild or severe; not many emotions are likely to emerge, although there may be some crying and other expressions of distress. Defences, especially of denial, will be high. Most will not ask for help although, depending on the incident, questions may be asked and feelings expressed concerning blame and guilt. If the police need to attend they will ask for statements to be made. This is best done on the premises rather than removing people to the police station—those who have suffered the traumatic incident need to be kept with their friends as much as possible. In some cases it helps to normalise reactions if people stay in the workplace where the incident happened. To remove them might suggest that they are sick or ill or will have problems when they return.

WHAT CAN MANAGERS AND SUPERVISORS DO?

Managers, supervisors and other senior members of staff should be aware that some police officers have a tendency to take over the situation and, because of the shock of the incident, managers may sometimes be only too happy to hand over their responsibility to them:

> 'Thank God the police are here to take over.'

Managers should not allow this to happen, but, where possible, should remain firmly in charge of their staff and let the police know this. Nothing should be done without the manager's or supervisor's permission—a situation like this should be avoided at all costs:

> Following an armed robbery the police came and immediately took away the young woman who had faced the robber. Within minutes, she was ushered into a police car and driven around the town and railway station in an attempt to find and identify the criminal. It was the middle of winter, she was in a state of shock and shivering with fear, and they didn't think to ask her to take a coat. She was even left in the car alone for some minutes.

Here the young and inexperienced police offers were acting with the best of intentions, but the victim was in no state to be treated in this way—her worst fear was that if the robber saw her he would shoot her. The manager should not have allowed her to be taken away, unless it was absolutely imperative, in which case she should have had a close friend or colleague with her.

Another reason why it is essential for managers to remain firmly in charge is that they need to retain, or regain, their self-confidence and the sense of control that has been taken from them by the robber and by the incident. Giving statements to the police can in fact be very helpful for both victims and witnesses, because it helps them to order things in their minds and to begin to put the ordeal into perspective. However, events such as identification parades and court cases can be extremely threatening because they tend to resurrect painful emotions. Furthermore, those taking part may feel exposed and vulnerable—the criminal sees them and identifies them, and there is always the fear of retaliation and revenge:

'He now knows me and will come and get me later.'

They also need to be aware of the effects on themselves. It is sometimes thought that traumatic incidents affect only ordinary members of staff, that managers and others in positions of authority should be able to cope. This is a myth, for in some ways they may be *more* affected than others. Part of the problem is that, being senior and usually more experienced, they are *expected* to be in charge and therefore to cope. But if for whatever reason they perceive themselves as not having coped well, they may experience strong feelings of failure and guilt:

'I was in charge, so it is my responsibility that this happened and I was unable to prevent it from happening. I felt so helpless and useless and couldn't protect my staff. Therefore I am to blame. I should have been better prepared and should have prepared my staff for it.'

Clearly, senior members of staff need to have a good understanding of what traumatic incidents may do, both to their staff and to themselves.

In order to be experienced as traumatic by those involved, an incident need not be so obviously violent and shock-inducing as a road accident or an armed robbery. The problem is that many different kinds of incident can cause traumatic reactions, and they need not be events that provide headline news. A distressing divorce, or something as seemingly simple as someone discovering that she was adopted, can be just as disturbing. Nor are people's reactions, either at the time or later, necessarily any indication of how they are coping. One cries and screams, while another stands around in silence keeping a stiff upper lip. It may be that the one who is coping best is the one who is screaming. Perhaps the other one is holding down his or her emotions, only for the reactions to emerge much later and when least expected.

Critical incident debriefing

Critical incident debriefing, also known as psychological debriefing, is a technique that can be used some two to three days after an incident, but it must be carried out only by a person who is trained to do it. This kind of debriefing is done either with an individual or with a group. It must not be done immediately after the incident or even the next day, because the initial reactions of those directly involved will usually be of shock, and in some cases denial will mean that they are heavily defended against accepting help. They may exist for a while in a state of limbo, doing their work correctly but behaving and feeling like robots. They may, alternatively, be 'on a high' and use humour to cope—especially black humour. It is only two or three days after the incident that most will feel able to sit down and talk about it in any logical way.

This kind of debriefing, which is a highly structured process, consists of the following stages:

Introduction The debriefer introduces himself and explains the rules and procedure.

Preparation The debriefer encourages the group or individual to outline what was happening immediately before the incident took place.

Stage 1: The facts This involves a highly detailed telling of the story by each person from beginning to end, but *without* any emotions being expressed. The focus is on what people thought and did.

The senses The debriefer asks about smells, sights, sounds, tastes and touches associated with the event. This is the trigger for moving on to Stage 2.

Stage 2: The feelings The participants are encouraged to talk about their feelings and emotional reactions and to identify where they each belong in the story. They are also asked to say how they feel about the incident now.

Stage 3: The future The debriefer aims to normalise reactions through reassurance and by giving a brief description of post-trauma stress. They are then encouraged to look at what resources are available to them should they need help—personal, group, organisational and external.

The whole procedure is rather like laying out a jigsaw on the table; then looking at the picture as a whole; breaking it up into its constituent pieces; then beginning to identify where the various feelings, sensations and emotional reactions—the 'pieces'—belong. The process is not counselling, but it gives people a better grasp of what has happened, helps them to make better sense of their experiences, enables them to share their reactions with others, and shows them that help is available should they need it. Most important of all, it shows them that they are normal people who have experienced an abnormal incident and that their reactions are normal.

Remember that the best way of helping those who suffer

from PTS reactions is to acknowledge and allow them to express their feelings. This means that you, the listener and helper, should know about reactions to trauma and attempt to normalise them rather than see them as signs of weakness or inadequacy. Never say:

> 'Control yourself and don't get upset. Don't cry or get angry. Be strong for other people. You mustn't blame anyone. It wasn't anybody's fault.'

Reactions such as these may make things worse. Moreover, they will suggest that the person speaking has no understanding of PTS reactions.

Help with trauma counselling may be sought from counsellors, psychologists, psychotherapists or psychiatrists, and referral may be made through the local GP.

6 Bullying

We usually associate bullying with children, either at school or at play, but bullying is common in the working environment. It has been estimated that over one-third of those away from work at any one time suffering from stress-related illnesses are ill because of bullying. As well as inducing illness, bullying is related to poor performance at work, low morale, lack of initiative and absenteeism, and so besides affecting working people and their environment it has some bearing on productivity and costs, thus ultimately affecting an organisation's financial success. Managers, supervisors and any who take the trouble to listen to others are almost certain, at some time, to come across bullying and harassment. They need to be aware of the methods of bullying used and of the symptoms and effects, and they must know what to do about it.

Harassment—from an Old French word for setting a dog on someone—as distinct from bullying, is usually defined as troubling or worrying someone. In other words, it means not leaving the target alone, but continually getting at him and being 'on his back' for some reason or other, or for none at all. 'Harass' is not unlike the word 'worry', which comes from an Old English word meaning 'to strangle', used in the sense of a dog 'worrying' a sheep.

Harassment is commonly associated with race and sex and is not usually as aggressive as bullying, although it can be just as distressing, even devastating, and have similar results. Racial harassment is more often verbal than physical in the working environment, and may include social segregation, the isolation of individuals or groups from others. Sexual harassment, in particular, considered to be common at work, is largely directed by men against women, although it can be by women against men. It may be explicitly and aggressively physical or take the form of displaying nude or provocative wall calendars, photographs or objects, or verbal innuendo. It may also crop up as requests for sexual favours in return for promotion or other benefits, or as a direct threat of dismissal or of adverse reports or assessments if the target does not comply. Sexual harassment may be typical of organisations that are largely male-dominated. It can be extremely upsetting for a woman to work in an environment where males are constantly making remarks about sex, about their sexual prowess or about her physical appearance. Sexual harassment can also take the seemingly 'harmless' form of brushing up against the person or touching her in a casual but deliberate manner. It may even result in rape. This kind of harassment can be seen as a form of bullying.

Bullying can be defined as 'the use of power in order to intimidate others', and has been called 'psychological terrorism'. The results of bullying are typical of the symptoms of stress and of post-trauma stress described in chapters 2 and 5, and can seriously influence health and relationships. Bullying can even result in breakdown, mental illness or suicide.

In a survey of workers by the University of Staffordshire it was discovered that:

53% surveyed had been bullied;
78% had witnessed bullying;
19% believed they had been the only one being bullied at the time it happened to them.

This suggests that more than half the workforce experience bullying at some level and at some time, that more than three-quarters witness it, and that bullies usually bully more than one person.

The typical bully has been described as 'a child dressed up as an adult'. Bullies have often been deprived as children, not necessarily through poverty, but more in terms of their relationships with parents, who may not have given them much love or security. They come from all walks of life and all classes. For whatever reasons, the typical bully has an inner need to be aggressive, to be sadistic, to harass, hurt and humiliate and to undermine others in whatever ways he or she can. These considerations should not be seen as attempts to excuse, for though we may try to understand the bully we must never accept his behaviour. As far as position is concerned, it is often the line manager or senior line manager who is the workplace bully, although anyone with power over others may resort to bullying.

TYPICAL BULLYING METHODS

Bullies operate in many ways, and will often use more than one strategy.

1 *Removing authority*

Someone in a responsible position may have her authority taken away from her so that she is no longer able to make decisions about people, about finance or about production. She may be moved from one job or department to another. This can be humiliating and may result in a loss of confidence and self-esteem, with consequent effects on efficiency and relationships both at work and at home.

2 *Intimidation and threat*

Such behaviour may be overt, or it may be insidiously covert and underhand. It can be carried out either publicly or privately in order to humiliate and hurt. It can be especially prevalent in a working and economic climate where redundancy and dismissal are common. If 78 per cent of people have witnessed bullying in the workplace, this suggests that bullies are not usually worried about their behaviour being seen. This may be because they believe that, when it is carried out in public, it enhances their image and power.

3　Creating uncertainty

This may be linked with (2) above, where there is fear and uncertainty about tenure of appointment and about possibilities of promotion (or fear of demotion). It may also involve threats concerning confidential reports or assessments. It can lead to the creation of an atmosphere of mistrust and general confusion, with people not knowing where they stand or where they can go for help, and this can destroy both individual and group morale. This strategy is often intended to disorientate and confuse.

4　Questioning competence

This is probably a necessary part of normal disciplinary procedure for maintaining quality and efficiency, but it becomes bullying when it is aggressive, sadistic or humiliating. The target is constantly having his abilities and performance criticised:

> The bully, who was a senior director, would send a note asking his secretary to do something. When she had finished the task he would go into her office and ask why she had done it. He would then shout and swear at her and throw things around, denying that he had asked her to do it. When she showed him the note he would tear it into shreds and continue his denial and the battery of abuse. This was extremely humiliating for the secretary, who was afraid to do anything in case she lost her job. The abusive language mainly concerned her competence and capabilities as a secretary.

5　Increasing workload beyond capabilities

The bully will purposely put pressure on individuals or groups by demanding a greater output than they can provide. This may lead to distress, anxiety, feelings of guilt and to further accusations of incompetence.

6　Specific threats of dismissal and redundancy

Common in all of the methods of bullying listed here, and especially effective and destructive in climates of high unemployment. Such threats are sometimes directed at people on their return to work when they have been off sick. They can also result from some real or imaginary mistake. They lead to verbal abuse and to the questioning of the ability and competence of the target.

7 Criticism

Sometimes delivered in front of others, criticism humiliates the recipient and stresses and confirms the power of the bully. It may be done openly, aggressively and violently and may be accompanied by shouting, swearing and threats. The opposite method—where the instigator calmly and quietly 'puts the individual down' and humiliates her, sometimes more by his silence and threatening looks or behaviour than by verbal aggression or criticism—is no less a form of bullying.

8 Verbal abuse

The bully may swear and shout and will sometimes pick on some aspect of the physical appearance of the individual, such as his colour, making it the object of the abuse. Alternatively, the focus may be a person's sex or beliefs, or some kind of physical or mental disability. It may be some facial or other feature—even something as simple as hairstyle or clothing. One young man was frequently abused verbally because he had long hair which he wore in a pony-tail. Verbal abuse also includes talking not to, but in front of, someone or a group about subjects that are offensive to them. The subject may again be the individual's appearance, or her intelligence or supposed lack of it, or her parentage, or it may be based on religion, politics, race or sex. Verbal abuse can also take the form of suggestive remarks and innuendoes.

9 Physical abuse

Bullies will frequently use physical abuse, although not necessarily through direct physical contact. It is often accomplished through extravagant and aggressive body language, and in violence against things rather than against people. There are many examples of individuals smashing furniture or throwing equipment around in front of those they are bullying (as we saw in (4) above). This strategy may also include hammering fists on desks, gesticulating wildly, tearing up files and letters, thrusting faces and heads close up, clenching teeth and staring hard, spitting at people or throwing things directly at them.

10   Regular humiliation
Bullying, which is meant to intimidate, hurt and humiliate and includes both direct and veiled insults against individuals or groups, may be all the more insidious when practised regularly. The instigator may use it every day, while another strategy is to do it irregularly so that the person bullied never knows when he will strike.

11   Initiation ceremonies
Although by definition not usually regularly inflicted on the same person, initiation ceremonies are often seen as methods of making outsiders acceptable to a closely knit specialist team or group. Sometimes they are quite harmless and do result in people acquiring a stronger sense of belonging. But they can also be sadistic and humiliating, and do not always result in acceptance either by the individual or the group. Some ceremonies may even be invented by the bully, especially if he or she is in a position of power.

12   Aggression
Like physical abuse, aggression is not always overtly physical. It can, for instance, be conducted silently. The bully might frequently brush up against an individual, thereby intimidating him or her—in a way that is defended as 'just being friendly' or 'just pushing past her [him]'.

13 Social rejection

Individuals, pairs or groups may simply be excluded from normal conversation or activities. This causes isolation and loneliness and the feeling of being an outcast. It can be extremely hurtful, and those bullied in this way will find it very difficult to survive in such an atmosphere. For those on the inside it can increase group solidarity and may create strong feelings of belonging, but this will only further isolate the ones being rejected.

Excuses made by bullies
When confronted with their behaviour, bullies may say:

'If he can't take a joke, he shouldn't have joined.'
'If she was doing her job properly it wouldn't have happened.'
'She needed to be shouted at because she was incompetent.'
'It wasn't meant to hurt anyone.'
'He's just taking it the wrong way.'
'I didn't mean anything by it. It was perfectly harmless.'
'I have no idea what you are talking about.'
'I'm in charge and I'll do what I like.'
'It's all a story made up by somebody who can't cope.'
'Nobody else has complained.'
'If you can't stand the heat, get out of the kitchen.'

Most of these are defences on the part of the bully. Such accusations against those being bullied—of incompetence, lack of humour, inadequacy, weakness, laziness or inability to join in with the others—are frequently encountered.

SIGNS OF BULLYING IN THE WORKPLACE

There are usually signs that bullying is taking place, and the supervisor or manager should be aware of the forms such clues may take. None of them in themselves automatically means that a bully is operating but, on the other hand, they might well be pointers.

1   *Absenteeism and sickness*

High levels of absenteeism in one department, or concerning just one person, may mean that bullying is taking place. An individual may frequently be sick and absent from work, for regular and short or for long periods of time. He may complain of non-specific illnesses such as stomach troubles, pains or tightness in the chest, depression or acute anxiety, inability to sleep or relax and headaches. Some bullying makes people frightened of returning to work, which can result in either anger or a withdrawal into self. Some may be frightened of leaving the house or of crowds—typical symptoms of both agoraphobia and claustrophobia. In fact, absenteeism may not be accompanied by sickness as such, but simply by anger, frustration and fear. The victim may even flatly refuse to return to work—rather like a child playing truant from school. In some cases people have left home saying they are going to work, but have not gone there and have not told their parents, partner or family.

2   *Reduction in efficiency or productivity*

A fall in productivity and efficiency, either of a group or of an individual, could mean that bullying is taking place. Since bullying usually causes people to be more anxious and frightened, they may not achieve their given 'stats' or output levels. It is easy to blame the individual or group concerned and claim that they are not working hard enough, but the supervisor or manager needs to ask, 'Why is this happening?' Those who are being bullied may tend to make more mistakes than normal and feel that they are failures. They may become either introverted and isolated or aggressive and angry with others, and show a lack of initiative or spontaneity. And the working atmosphere may be one of dullness and deadness.

3 High staff turnover

If people are being bullied, they will, if they can, either resign or ask to be moved to another part of the workplace. They may not give their real reasons, but speak of the need for a change of environment or a change of colleagues, or of new interests and the desire to increase skills, expertise and experience. The urge to move may be due to bullying by either an individual or a group. Where people are regularly asking for transfers or leaving employment, this could be a pointer to bullying. It might be useful to note who are *not* asking for transfers or leaving and what positions they occupy, bearing in mind that, as mentioned earlier, the individual bully is often the line manager, senior line manager or some other person in a position of power. It might even be that a hierarchy of bullying is in operation, with a senior manager bullying a junior manager or supervisor who, in turn, bullies others.

4 Low morale and lack of team spirit

If bullying *is* at issue, it may affect not only the individual or individuals being bullied, but also the team or group to which they belong. People may feel that they have to concentrate on the work on their desks or benches rather than on the aspects of their job that involve them with colleagues, and they may be intimidated to such an extent that they isolate themselves. This will obviously affect relationships in the team, and may result in a lowering of morale and a reduction of team spirit. It will also influence production.

WHAT CAN THE VICTIM DO?

One major problem for the victim, as we have seen, is fear: fear of being made to look either a fool or a liar, especially in front of others; fear of reprisals by the bully; fear of rejection or hostility from colleagues; fear of being sacked or made redundant; fear of further bullying or of sexual or other physical harassment; fear of not knowing what to do or where to go for help. Perhaps the main problems are the fear of not being believed—'Nobody will believe me'—and the amount of physical and moral courage and conviction it takes to stand up and say, 'I am being bullied.'

The bully purposely causes fear, confusion and disorientation so that his target will not know where to turn or what to do. And the one on the receiving end may begin to believe that she deserves it and that it must be her own fault. She may even believe that it cannot be happening and begin to doubt her own sanity:

> 'Is it really happening? Should I tackle the bully myself or should I tell someone? If so, who shall I tell—my colleagues, or a superior, or someone else?'

These may be the reasons why some people endure bullying for so long.

Confrontation and assertiveness
One way of dealing with bullying is to tackle the bully directly. But it is better for the person concerned not to ask why he or she is doing it, as this 'puts the ball in his or her court'. The target of the bullying should state clearly what has been happening, saying that he will not put up with it. This confrontational approach may work, but it requires a great deal of courage and there are various possible outcomes. It may achieve the aim of stopping the bully, it may meet with denial or further aggression or, if the bully is in a position of power, it may elicit bad reports and eventual dismissal.

The secret is to respond assertively rather than aggressively. In order to do this, the person being bullied needs to have strong self-esteem and to really believe that he deserves respect and to be treated correctly. Low self-esteem usually results in aggression, anger and a failure to stop the bullying. Even when an individual knows that he has been bullied, it is often easier for him to think that he must have made a mistake. The trouble is that people who are bullied usually do have, or develop, a low estimate of their own worth. No matter what has happened, and even if people have made serious mistakes, they do not deserve to be bullied.

HOW DOES THE VICTIM KNOW THAT HE OR SHE IS BEING BULLIED?

Those who believe that they are being bullied need to ask themselves:

'Am I being bullied and why is it that I think I am? What evidence do I have that will convince others?'

Keep a diary with the following information:

- The exact dates and times when you were bullied.
- Details of what happened, where it happened and what was said and/or done.
- How you felt at the time.
- Whether or not there were any witnesses (with a record of names).
- Details of which witnesses are willing to report what they saw.

The bully's strategies outlined on pages 95–9 will be a useful guide, and if you recognise your situation in any of these, then you are probably being bullied.

There are other questions that you might ask:

- 'Do I feel that I am constantly being "got at" for no real reason, that I am being harassed?'
- 'Do I feel decidedly uncomfortable in my relationship with this person [the bully or suspected bully] as it now is, and has my relationship with him [her] changed? Does he [she] now treat me in a different way?'
- (if the bully or suspected bully is a new manager, super-visor or colleague) 'Is the relationship different from the previous one, and in what ways?'

- 'Do I wonder if the bullying I am receiving, in whatever form, is really my fault, and am I questioning my own judgement and competence because of it? Do I know that I am not at fault and that I have not changed in any way?'

The main question to ask is:

- 'Is the way I am being treated sadistic, aggressive, hurtful, humiliating and undeserved, and do I feel that I am being bullied?'

It is common for people who *are* being bullied not to say anything about it, to keep it to themselves. This only makes matters worse, unless the bully eventually directs his or her attentions elsewhere. But even here, although it may stop the bullying for the person in question, it does not stop the bully's activities, and he will simply look for someone who will respond more satisfactorily to his tactics. So the 'I will ignore it and they will stop' approach is likely to be only partially successful.

If the decision is that action is to be taken, there must be a carefully planned procedure rather than a response based on a 'gut reaction'. The gut reaction usually ends in more anger and confrontation, with the risk of the anger being directed at the bully in the form of violence—which could result in dismissal.

A plan of action
The individual who is being bullied should find the following suggestions helpful:

- Cultivate in yourself a firm sense of injustice about the way you are being treated, and an equally firm desire to put it right.
- Be determined to stop the bullying, and do not prevaricate or be evasive or unsure about what you wish to say and achieve.
- Know exactly what has happened to you, when and where you were bullied, and be quite clear about it in

your mind. Be prepared to give the bully a list of dates, times and places from a diary so that he will know that you are serious about it, and to present him with a copy.

- If necessary, rehearse what you want to say. Write it down so that it is clear in your mind. You can rehearse in front of a mirror or with a colleague or partner in a role-play.
- Choose the right time to speak. This might be when the bullying starts again or when the bully least expects you to tackle him.
- Consider having a colleague with you when you speak to the bully.
- When you speak, you can be angry inside, but be calm, clear and precise about what you have to say and in the way that you say it. Tell the bully exactly what he has been doing to you.
- Do not allow the bully to put you off by talking, shouting or denying. If you are attacked verbally, do not shout back, but state calmly and firmly that you will not tolerate being treated like this; and that, if necessary, you will call on some other authority—your union, or your welfare, personnel or occupational health officer, for instance. You might even say that you will make a formal complaint according to the procedure laid down by the organisation—after you have checked that there *is* such a procedure.
- Try to be confident about your own capabilities and judgement, and do not allow the bully to put you off your stroke.
- If he replies by making accusations against you about your competence or your ability, demand that he write it down.
- If there are witnesses who are willing to give evidence for you, say so, but do not give names at this stage.
- If the bully continues to deny his behaviour or keeps repeating that you have made a mistake or are exaggerating, say clearly that you have not made a mistake, that

you will not allow it to happen again, and that you are going to take the matter further.

- If it is a matter of racial or sexual harassment or bullying, you can mention the appropriate agency (see page 256).

Above all, the target of the bullying should not accept excuses or denial or a promise that it will stop and that the bully will not do it again, unless it was an isolated minor incident. Bullies do not often change their behaviour so quickly. The individual must be prepared to take the matter as high as he needs to in order to stop this particular bullying episode and to change the bully's behaviour. Even if he stops bullying his present victim, he will probably have no difficulty in finding others.

WHAT CAN MANAGERS AND SUPERVISORS DO?

In the mind of the manager, supervisor, welfare officer or colleague (or whoever is listening to the account) may arise the thought:

'Is this imaginary, or is it just a misunderstanding?'

But these are questions that should *not* be directed at an individual who says that she is being bullied. All accusations must be taken seriously. The first thing to do is to look for the possible signs of bullying mentioned on pages 99–101. This may give some indication of the atmosphere within the work environment. However, bullies often conduct their work in secret and some employees will not wish to acknowledge what they know is happening, either to themselves or to others.

When someone comes to you claiming that he is being bullied by another member of staff, you must be clear about what you should do and how you should do it:

- Ensure that you interview him in private and not in front of others—it should be somewhere safe where you will not be disturbed.

- State clearly that it is not your place to take sides, but that you are ready and willing to listen.
- Accept what you are being told. It is not a matter of believing or disbelieving, but of accepting it at face value. You are not a judge sitting in a court, and the accusations may or may not be true.
- Do not say that it could have been a mistake or a joke that went wrong, or that he may be exaggerating or have taken it out of all proportion. Even if you know the accused person well, do not try to defend him or her or to make excuses. It is easy to take sides with people you know, like or respect, whether the accuser or the accused.
- Do not dominate the session, and use your listening skills to the full—these skills will help him to be more precise.
- Take accurate and clear notes of what you are told—they may be needed later if the matter is taken further.
- Ask for details of times and places and ask if there were any witnesses and if you can have their names. You also need to know if this is the first time or if there have been other incidents, and when and where they occurred.
- Ask for details of exactly what happened. Try to get him to be precise, and do not accept vague accusations and suggestions. The problem here is that often people will not be clear, and may respond with uncertainty, tears and anger. They may even be frightened and embarrassed, or disgusted with themselves for not being able to cope. Again, patient use of listening skills will help.
- Ask if he has spoken to anyone else about it and, if so, to whom.
- Ask for details of his reactions, and how the incident affected him at the time.
- Ask how it has affected him since, both at work and at home. Have there been any effects on his relationships with others?
- If there is physical evidence of bullying ask to see it, unless it is personal or embarrassing. Has he been to the doctor, and is there any medical evidence available?

At the end of the session, give him a clear summary of what has happened in the interview, using the summarising skills outlined on pages 201–8. If the company or organisation has a definite procedure for dealing with such complaints, explain it. Then ask him if he wishes to take the matter further, and if he does, tell him exactly what courses of action are available. To make vague promises that something will be done is insufficient. Neither is it adequate to say that the bully will be spoken to and told to stop it. If there is a clearly laid-down procedure, it should be strictly adhered to.

- Reassure the person making the accusations that what he has said will be taken seriously and will not make any difference to his position at work. If possible, there should be no further direct or personal contact between the bully and the accuser. If this cannot be avoided, then a third party, such as a welfare or personnel officer, should be present.
- If bullying is admitted or proved, the bully should be disciplined according to company policy and, if possible, transferred to another area or department. Steps should also be taken to see that if the bully does not change his or her behaviour he or she is dismissed. This, of course, is extremely difficult if the bully happens to be the managing director or in some other very senior position.

Action should be taken as soon as possible—which is much easier if there is a laid-down procedure. It may be that the procedure is to see the bully and hear his or her side of the story, but the one receiving the complaint should not become an arbitrator or mediator between the bully and the one being bullied. The strategy of placating everyone involved and trying to maintain peace does not usually stop bullying, although it may act as a warning, inducing him or her to stop it for a short time. But the behaviour may then continue as before. In addition to the implementation of company procedures, external organisations may be called in to give help and advice to all parties, including the accused.

Bullying in the workplace must never be accepted as normal behaviour, no matter who the perpetrator may be—supervisor, managing director, or whoever. Partly because bullying often comes from high up, it is often difficult to prove that it has been or is taking place—which puts an extra burden on the victim, who may feel extremely vulnerable and exposed both in the working environment and outside it. Colleagues may not be as supportive as they could be because of their own fears about what might happen if they get involved. Bullying and harassment can be very isolating experiences, and it may even be necessary to remove people from the workplace while investigations are taking place.

Wherever it occurs, bullying must be dealt with—for all the reasons outlined in this chapter. At its worst, it can reduce what should be a happy and stimulating environment to a place of suspicion, anger and misery, not just for those being bullied, but for everyone.

PART TWO:
THE ART OF LISTENING

7   Getting to Know Yourself

If we are to learn to listen it is important to know something about ourselves and about what listening does to us and why. We can begin by looking at our own 'hidden agenda'—those parts of us that are hidden away and that influence our decisions and relationships and, therefore, the way we listen and respond to others.

Think of a problem—a fairly serious one—a personal problem from your own life or from the life of someone you know. Then decide that you have to go and talk to someone about it and seek their help. Look at the following list and pick *one* person that you feel you would be able to speak to about the problem. Pick only one, and stay with that choice:

Dr Abraham Mendelbaum MRCPsych.	psychiatrist
Ms Joan Armstrong	psychotherapist
The Rev Brian Williams MA BD	Baptist minister
Mr Salim Jafed BA CQSW	social worker
Mrs Anthea Cartier-Fitzwilliams	private counsellor
Dr Richard Simpson	doctor (GP)
Father Sean O'Flaherty SJ	Jesuit priest

First, ask yourself why you have chosen this particular person rather than any of the others. Second, go through the others on the list one by one and decide why you would not choose them. Did you make your particular choice because

1   you liked or preferred the name and qualifications?
2   you liked or preferred the job description?

Possible response:

'I chose Ms Joan Armstrong because I liked the sound of her name. It feels solid and down-to-earth and the 'Ms' means that she knows exactly where she stands and is quite strong-willed and forthright. Also, I know some psychotherapists and I believe that I could trust her to help me.'

Perhaps you rejected one of the others because

1   you disliked his or her title (Rev, Dr, Father, Ms, etc.)?
2   you disliked the person's name (e.g., Cartier-Fitzwilliams)?
3   you were not happy about the occupation (minister, priest, psychiatrist)?

Possible response:

'Well, I've nothing against Jewish people—I presume Dr Mendelbaum is Jewish—but I am wary of psychiatrists. I don't want to be labelled a psychiatric case. Anyway, I don't want to see a 'shrink'. The Baptist minister would probably throw the Bible at me and tell me to go to church or say my prayers. He's likely to be narrow-minded as well, so I wouldn't choose him. The social worker sounds foreign and I'm not too sure about social workers anyway. They have a bad image at present. They tend to be a bit scruffy and left-wing so I wouldn't go to him. I wouldn't go to the private counsellor because I don't like her name. Cartier-Fitzwilliams sounds upper-class and she's probably one of the 'twin-set and pearls brigade' who wouldn't understand an ordinary person like me. If I know anything of doctors it's that they never have time to listen. The GP would probably be looking at the notes of the next person on his list and have his pen poised over the prescription pad. I've nothing against Roman Catholics, but I think that Father O'Flaherty would try to convert me. Anyway, I've not had anything to do with priests and don't know if I could trust him to be impartial.'

So your choice depends to some extent on your previous experiences, ideas and beliefs as well as on your prejudices and preferences, and on your images of the listeners/helpers available. It also depends on the nature of the problem. It isn't much use going to the Baptist minister if you've broken your leg, or to the GP if you have a problem with a religious fanatic in your workplace.

Possible descriptions of the candidates:

Dr Mendelbaum is an Austrian Jewish psychiatrist. He is a gentle and kindly man with a wealth of experience who would listen carefully to you and do what he could to help—*or*—Dr Mendelbaum speaks little English and with a strong German accent, and he is a Freudian who believes that all your problems are down to sex and would put you into a psychiatric pigeon-hole.

Ms Armstrong is a single parent who is quite strong-minded; she is trained to listen carefully and has wide experience of many different aspects of life—*or*—Ms Armstrong is a hard-line feminist who hates men, so if you are a man, don't bother going. If you are a woman, and especially a married woman, she will despise you.

The Rev Brian Williams is fairly liberal in his views and is a Relate-trained and -experienced counsellor with a breadth of expertise and experience from which to draw—*or*—the Rev Brian Williams is a biblical fundamentalist and would try to convert you to his beliefs and give you religious tracts to read.

Mr Jafed was born in London and comes from a wealthy Asian family who sent him to public school; because of his training and experience, if he couldn't help . e would direct you to someone who could—*or*—Mr Jafed speaks little Engiish and works entirely with the immigrant community.

Mrs Cartier-Fitzwilliams is a highly qualified counsellor who has dealt over the last thirty years with a vast range of problems—*or*—Mrs Cartier-Fitzwilliams is an upper-middle-class snob who thinks that she knows how to solve people's problems; she believes that the solution to most difficulties is to pull yourself together.

Dr Simpson is a GP who sets aside one afternoon each week for people who want more of his time than he is able to give in normal surgery hours; he also has a counsellor on his staff—*or*—Dr Simpson is too busy to give you more than five minutes of his time, and he never really listens.

Father O'Flaherty is a broad-minded, gentle southern-Irish priest who will sit and listen to you with great attention and try to help you to work through your problems— *or*—Father O'Flaherty is a hard-liner who believes that the only solution is for you to become a devout Roman Catholic.

As you read this, you may be reacting strongly to some of these descriptions. The important thing is to realise that even before we meet people we already have a vast store of information and experience, both good and bad, packed away in our minds. We meet someone for the first time and, for no apparent reason, don't like him or her. We meet someone else and immediately there is an attraction we can't explain and we get on 'like a house on fire'. With others, we may have to wait before we can decide whether or not we like them. Sometimes we say that we take people at face value, but experience of them may then teach us that we can't trust them or that we can't get on with them. On the other hand, we may simply learn to tolerate them, especially if we have to work with them.

Why *is* it that we don't get on with some people and yet we do with others? There are innumerable possible answers. But consider the following exercise—I have done it with groups on a number of occasions and the results are surprising.

Take a large group of people who do not know each other, and imagine them following these instructions:

'Walk around the room in complete silence and look at each other. In your own time choose a partner who reminds you of someone from your past, someone you think you could get on with. Then sit with her in silence and work out what she may be like as a person—what character or personality, hobbies or interests, she may have. After a reasonable length of time tell each other what you have worked out about the other. Then discuss it and see how right or wrong you were. Go on to talk to each other about your backgrounds. Then check out what each of you has said, how accurate you each were and what you have in common.'

The remarkable thing about this exercise is how often people seem to find someone who 'fits' them and how often they get the information about him or her right. Obviously, people do not normally say objectionable things about each other on first meeting, and they tend to be generous in their estimates, but what they seem to guess and discover about their partners in this exercise can often be a bit 'spooky'.

What appears to happen is that, right from the beginning when they are moving around in silence, people are already choosing a partner from his or her body language and looks. And they also sometimes choose someone who has a similar psychological background to their own, and who, it turns out, in important ways mirrors their own past and present life experiences. The chosen person will often 'fit' not just the chooser's own personality, but also his or her specific likes and dislikes. It is an unconscious as well as conscious process—at the time, they are not necessarily aware of why they choose this other person. As they walk around there are hidden factors at work and, consciously and unconsciously, they are making judgements and choices about the other people. Each person will be attracted to some and feel neutral towards others, and there will be some whom they don't like or are not quite sure about.

In a recent exercise with twenty-four people, they all chose a partner and there were many similarities in the pairs. The last couple to pair off were two men, who were slightly angry and said that since their partner was the only one left, neither of them had had any choice in the matter. When asked what they had in common they said that there were no similarities whatsoever, either in their lives or in their characters. When pressed further they both said, 'We have nothing at all in common.' After a brief silence, one of them added, 'Except that our parents divorced when we were both seven years old.'

Perhaps it is too easy to suggest that, for these two, feelings of rejection were so liable to be aroused that they felt threatened by the group, and so both unconsciously chose not to choose someone. By doing so, by not choosing, they actually did choose someone similar to themselves. And what happened was that they stayed together for the rest of the course.

One simple way of looking at this is via 'the iceberg theory' (see Figure 4).

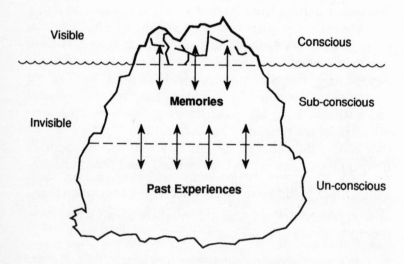

Figure 4. The iceberg theory.

THE ICEBERG THEORY

Imagine that every human being is like an iceberg floating around in the sea of life. Only a small part is visible above the water. Most of the iceberg is hidden away from view, and these hidden parts lie at various depths.

On the surface is the *conscious* part—what can be seen by other icebergs as they float around in the sea. We can instantly recall our own names and birthdays. Just below the surface is the *subconscious*, in which lie our more recent experiences and memories. (It takes a little longer to recall what we had for lunch yesterday or what we did last week or last month. And we all have the experience of knowing the answer to a quiz question, but being unable to recall it when needed.) At a deeper level still lie our *unconscious* memories and experiences. Some of them we think we have forgotten, but a photograph, a person's name, a smell or a sound, and it all comes flooding back into consciousness:

> 'Once when I was visiting my parents, my father said that a man who had been at school with me over forty years ago had died. When his name was mentioned, I could see his face and even hear his voice. It all came rushing back from the depths of my mind. I would never have remembered his name had I been asked, 'Guess who has just died and was at school with you.'

Deep down there are memories that we do not wish to remember and have buried away and, we think, forgotten. Sometimes, the more painful the memories are, the deeper we bury them and cover them over with a protective shell. Difficult childhood experiences, broken relationships, experiences of fear or rejection, things we have done of which we are ashamed or upsetting things that others have done to us—all this we prefer to forget. On the other hand, we also have good experiences buried away, and these too can be forgotten and yet influence the present:

'I know that I was wanted and loved as a child and that my parents showed warmth and affection to each other and to me. I also know that I was accepted just as I was, unconditionally, and did not face criticism or abuse and that I felt, and still feel, secure. I have a positive self-image and high self-esteem. I feel loved and, above all, lovable.'

Some people have difficulty in giving love to others, and this may be because they feel unlovable. To feel unlovable is not the same as feeling unloved. If I see myself as unlovable, it means that I believe deep down inside that nobody can really love me, even if they tell me and show me that they do. Because of what I feel about myself inside, perhaps unconsciously, and because my experience in my formative years has been of not being loved, I may also find it difficult to give love.

Of course, it is possible that those on whom I would like to focus love are not particularly nice, or that I happen to be in a bad mood or feeling unwell. But if my feeling unlovable and my difficulty in giving love are states with which I am all too familiar, it may be to do with how I basically feel about myself and how I see myself in my self-image. The problem is that as a child it was impossible for me to view life or myself in an 'adult' way. If I was abused, or left for long periods of time—if my mother went away or into hospital when I was very young—then the conclusion I drew was that it must have been because I was bad. I may have been (may still be) unable to say that my parents were bad or express my anger and frustration:

'It has to be my fault, and I am to blame.'

I projected inside myself the feelings of badness or isolation that should rightly have been directed at others, and I came to the conclusion that nobody could ever love me.

Some of the bad experiences are very much part of our consciousness. We live with them every day and they affect how we feel, how we are and how we behave. For example, if I was abused or neglected as a child, this experience may be an ever-present reality for me and I may be fully aware of how it influences my behaviour and reactions, especially towards others. On the other hand, there are experiences that have affected me but that I cannot consciously remember. With a skilled counsellor or therapist they might begin to come to the surface—I might gradually be brought to realise what they are, where they come from and how they are affecting me and my relationships with others:

> Angela came to see me because she was becoming increasingly frightened of death and of dying. She was twenty-two years old, happily married, and had a good job which she enjoyed. But she was just terrified of dying and had this intense fear most of the time. At our meeting she burst into tears—she did not know why she was so afraid of dying, but it was seriously impinging on her life. She was having intrusive thoughts during the day, and her sleep was full of nightmares about dying. We talked for some time, and then I asked her about her childhood and family life. She said that she had had wonderful parents who were loving and caring. However, when we dug deeper, this turned out to be something of a fantasy. Her father was often away from home because of his work, and he believed strongly that people had to learn to cope on their own. He had been put into a children's home when he was little, and had struggled hard throughout his life to survive. Eventually, Angela was able to recall vividly that when she was about four or five, and cried or went to him with her problems, he had told her regularly that you just had to get on with life and cope. You were on your own, and you would die alone. Even if others were with you, you would die alone. She said, 'He told me this over and over again. I was being bullied regularly at school—you see, I was always little and very ugly when I was a child.' In fact, she was an attractive woman and had been a pretty little girl.

The feelings associated with these events from her childhood had been well hidden away, but had been triggered when a neighbour, who was a religious fanatic, told her that one day she would die and be all alone facing God, and if she didn't believe what he believed she would go to hell. At that point she had not been able consciously to remember where her reactions and emotions came from. It was only when, through counselling, she was able to identify their source that she gradually learned to face them and to cope. She was reassured to know that she was not stupid or going mad, and she was also able to examine for herself what she could really accept about God.

This case seems to show that, from deep inside the iceberg, the messages emerging from the past were influencing how the subject thought and felt about herself. They had also determined, to some extent, how she reacted and behaved towards others.

Let's take the iceberg image further. Here we are, icebergs in the sea of life, and as we drift towards each other what we all see is the ice above the water. We make our judgements and decisions on this bit that we can see, but the first parts of us that actually make contact are well beneath the surface. We icebergs collide at a deep level, crunching and grinding against each other. Unknown to us, our subconscious and unconscious levels are meeting and inter-reacting. Hence our feeling that we like this person rather than that one, but without being aware of the reasons. This person 'fits' in some way with our subconscious and unconscious past experiences. That person we dislike on sight, we can't get on with him, but we don't know why. At an under-the-surface level we are somehow aware of what different individuals are like inside, and our past experiences and theirs are reaching out and meeting each other— or, alternatively, recoiling.

So the 'hidden agenda', which we all have, is a vast store of information, experiences and emotional reactions at different levels in our minds. And all of these, with our present experiences, combine to make us what we are, what we think and believe and what we like and dislike in ourselves and in other people. Our thoughts and feelings emerge from deep inside the iceberg, influencing our attitudes towards ourselves and others. Of course, our reactions and feelings will be influenced by other things as well, both internal and external. We might be unwell, tired and sad, or elated. We will also be affected by other people's body language—what we see and then interpret from the way they stand or sit, from the expressions on their faces, from the way they move their eyes, their hands, their whole body. Body language can tell us a great deal about others, but our interpretations are our own and are the result of our own internal 'bits', our hidden agenda.

Thus, the iceberg theory can throw light on why we behave as we do, as well as on the lives of those around us. The light is not just in my eyes, for, if I am a good listener, I see people beginning to understand themselves better and being able to relate their past to their present. If we *can* see what we are now, where this comes from and how the two fit together, we are some way along the road to self-understanding. And if we can begin to understand ourselves, then perhaps we can begin to understand other people.

Getting to know ourselves and getting to know others are two processes that go on in tandem, for we do not live in isolation like Robinson Crusoe before Man Friday came along. Our lives are interwoven with each other in the present as well as, to some extent, determined by our past. It is rather like being in a time warp: there is no such thing as the present, for the past hurtles along behind us and pushes us into the future. No sooner have we thought about the present than it is gone and has become the past. Meanwhile, we need to know and feel that we can, in some measure, be in control of our lives. And knowing more of what we are and why we behave as we do will not only help us to understand and relate to others in a more positive way, it will also make us better listeners.

8 The Helper

What can we do as helpers and carers? What kind of help can we give to people who are in need or who seek our assistance and advice?

We can offer any of the following:

1 Information

Information usually takes the form of instructions, and is handed out by somebody who knows, or thinks she knows, something that you don't know. It can be as simple as, 'Go down there and turn right. Take the second left, and the post office is on the right of the bus station.' Information may be correct or it may not be. The practice of giving it is a very useful one, for we all rely on information from other people and from other sources such as newspapers, radio, television, books, maps, leaflets, letters and magazines. Information can help us not only to know what to do but also where to go for further help. Organisations like the Citizens' Advice Bureaux are experts in giving information.

2 Advice

There is an old riddle, 'What is it we all like to give but never take?' The answer is 'Advice'. What this normally involves is us telling others what we think they should do. It is usually based on our experiences, and is what we would probably do if we were in their shoes. Often we value advice from people we respect and admire, and sometimes it can be helpful. We will look at advice later, and at some of the problems it can present.

3 Opinions

Sometimes a friend will say to us, 'What do you think I should do?' It is quite flattering to be asked for our opinion. Although it can be difficult to know what to say, especially when the friend has a problem and doesn't know what to do, it can make us feel valued and important. However, our opinion may prove worthless, we may make things worse by expressing it, and he may then blame us for the result. Later in this chapter, we look at the problems that giving opinions can raise.

4 Understanding

We can offer ourselves as caring people and hope to show a person with a problem that we are compassionate and understanding, as well as helping her to see the way through her problem. If we can help her to know more about her feelings and situation we may help her to move forward in her life. It can sometimes be helpful, if you have had a similar problem, for the other person to know that you share something of what she has experienced. But remember that the fact that you have had a similar experience or problem does not mean that your experience or problem was the same as hers. We can never really understand how another person feels—we sometimes don't even understand our own feelings. We are different people and will react in some ways that are similar and in others that are different.

5 Communication

Sometimes we may be placed in the position of mediator between two or more people. We may be able to help them to communicate with each other better and to work through disagreement, misunderstanding or conflict more effectively. We can also convey information between different groups and individuals—this could be as simple as letting a manager know how his employees feel and taking information back to them.

6   Support

It may be that we can do little other than just be there with the troubled person. Standing or sitting beside him or holding his hand can give support and be very reassuring. We should never underestimate the value of this, especially when, desperate to help and find some solution, we can do nothing else. When someone is anxious or worried, upset or ill, unconscious or dying, holding his hand or just a touch may be all that we can offer, but it may be just what is needed. A word of reassurance, when appropriate, can also help.

7   Action

In difficult situations we tend to be very keen to *do something*. We must be seen to be helping. Giving practical assistance is often useful, and we believe it to be the sign of a good neighbour or citizen. However, we must be sure not to take away a person's self-esteem or confidence by doing things he can do for himself. Driving you to the railway station may be helpful, but it may not be helpful if I do something for you that you can do for yourself. When someone has died it is easy to say: 'I'll do everything for you so that you don't have to worry.' The point is that the bereaved often need to do things like arranging the funeral and sorting out the dead person's affairs because they need to feel involved in what has happened. It can help them to move through the process of grieving (see Chapter 4). Action should not override a person's capacity to help himself.

8   Influence

Exerting any influence we may have can be very useful. It may, for instance, be a question of helping those in authority to make what we believe to be the right decisions about a problem. We can sometimes bring about changes in rules and regulations, or use whatever power we have to adjust or adapt them as necessary. This is not usually easy to do, and raises questions about the use of power and about policies and politics. We may be afraid of those who seek to change things and see them as left- or right-wing activists, a threat to the safety and security of our lives and to the status quo. It can be helpful to others when we use our influence constructively, but it can raise issues about what is right or wrong. All the same, we usually feel good when we can 'bend the rules' to help someone.

These are eight things, then, that we can do, but what kind of person do you have to be in order to be an effective helper? 'Doing' is very practical, but what about 'being'?— because to some extent, as mentioned earlier, what you do is based on what you are.

Hugh Eadie, in an article on stress among clergy,[1] describes the typical helper as someone who has an idealised self-image, who feels guilty and is self-critical, has a compulsive–obsessive personality, tends to control his or her sexual impulses, is passive and conforming, attempts to resolve conflicts, tends towards self-hatred and shows symptoms of stress. You may say, 'That's me all right', or, alternatively, you may feel that such characteristics would tend to belong to a person who would be totally unsuited to helping others. It is comforting to know that Eadie goes on to say that his profile does not necessarily represent destructive or even adverse criticism of helpers, but that these characteristics tend to be the basis for an effective, caring personality. If he is right, though, it does mean that carers and helpers need to be aware of their own hang-ups so that these do not get in the way of their helping.

THE PERSON-CENTRED APPROACH

Carl Rogers, the exponent on the person-centred approach to helping and counselling, speaks of three basic personal qualities necessary in the good helper:

[1] Eadie, 'Clergy stress', *Contact*, 1975.

1   Genuineness

We know what we mean when we say, 'He's a genuine person', but it is difficult to say exactly what it means. Genuineness is a self-awareness that enables the helper to relate to the other person as a real human being; there is no hiding behind an assumed role or uniform. It is easy to use our position as manager or supervisor, or as policeman, doctor or priest, as a barrier in order to protect ourselves from getting too deeply involved or from coming too close to another person or situation. You can hide very effectively behind a white coat, dog-collar or even a secretary. Buildings and organisations may create the same effect. Walking into a hospital can be an unnerving and frightening experience, for we are entering what is for most of us an alien and unknown world. We may have the same feeling when entering the manager's or supervisor's office.

So the carer and helper needs to be someone who is open and honest about himself, devoid of delusions, and aware of his own reactions and feelings. He should also know what the other person is likely to feel when faced by him and *his* surroundings.

2   Acceptance

Carl Rogers speaks of caring about others so much that you 'prize' them and treat them as precious and unique. This approach is about valuing the other person as an individual, no matter what you may feel or believe about her. You may dislike her intensely and hate what she has done or the situation she is in. You may not agree with her values, standards, beliefs or behaviour, but you accept her just as she is, 'warts and all'. The person-centred approach means being non-judgemental in the way we present ourselves and behave, even though we may make our own internal judgements; and it means treating the other person as though she matters because we believe that she really is of value and importance.

3 Empathy

This is not to be confused with sympathy (see page 135), although there is a clear similarity. A dictionary definition of sympathy states that it is the ability to share another person's feelings, or a feeling of tenderness towards someone suffering pain or grief. The word comes from the Greek, meaning 'feeling with'. We often use it in this way:

'I sympathise with you because I've been through the same thing myself. I know how you feel.'

We also use it in the sense of feeling sorry for someone.

The word 'empathy' is defined as the power to identify mentally with and comprehend another person and his situation. It literally means 'feeling in' or 'in-feeling'. When we empathise we try to put ourselves into another person's world, to be inside his skin without losing sight of the fact that the experience is that person's and not ours. We begin to move under the umbrella of the other person's world—or, putting it another way, we move out from under our umbrella to stand with him in the rain:

When I visited Canada I went to a place called Medicine-Hat and found a shop selling parchments billed as 'Old Indian proverbs'. One said, 'Pass judgement on no man until you have walked two moons in his moccasins.' This seemed to cover both acceptance and empathy, but I did note that on the back of the parchment it said, 'Made in Hong Kong'!

This proverb, whether American Indian or not, goes to the heart of the attitude that we should develop and show towards others. Without it, we may ride roughshod over them, believing that we know what's best for them and can tell them what to do. We may do this without having the slightest idea of what their real situation is or what they are feeling. This can result in the loss of the credibility of the helper, who may well also lose the trust of the person he is trying to help, and may even turn a problem into a disaster.

Rogers argued that, for a helper, listener or counsellor to be effective, these three 'client-contact skills' are essential. It may well be that the way that anyone responds, whether as helper or counsellor, to someone asking for help, is directly related to the degree of self-understanding shown by the client. When the helper reflects feelings that she perceives in her client, the client is able to explore himself and his life more fully. But when the helper offers value judgements, opinions or interpretations, it seems that the client stops self-exploration. The trouble is that when the helper gives opinions and advice and makes judgements, the focus of the session moves from the person with the problem to the helper. It cannot be stressed too often that listeners need to learn to listen before they speak, so that when they do speak it is with a sound knowledge of the other person and his problems. Furthermore, when the listener reflects on what her client has said and feeds it back to him, they are both able to explore his situation further and to derive a better understanding of what the problems are. When I am helping you, my feelings, prejudices, preferences, ideas and beliefs are important to me, but they may not be of much use or interest to you.

To some extent, therefore, the direction of the helping process is influenced not only by the self-understanding shown by the client, but also by the self-understanding shown by the helper or listener. Eugene Kennedy's book, *On Becoming a Counsellor*[2] is very much more about the counsellor and listener than about clients and their problems. This is as it should be—as already noted, listeners need to look closely at the hidden areas of their own lives, and to ask questions such as:

[2] Kennedy, E. *On Becoming a Counsellor*, Dublin: Gill & Macmillan, 1990.

- What are my own problems, and how do they influence my attitudes towards others?
- In what ways does this person facing me affect me and influence me?
- What do I think and feel about her problems, and how does this affect how I respond?
- Which bits of me determine what I will say and do?

HOW CAN THE HELPER RESPOND?

Perhaps we are most likely to offer advice, opinions, sympathy and practical help:

1 Advice
This usually takes the form of:

'The best thing you can do is . . .'

or

'I think you should . . .'

Example:

'Should I pack in my job and go back to college?'
'The best thing you can do is to stay with your work, especially when so many people are unemployed.'

The trouble is that I, the helper, do not know what you, the person with the problem, should do in your situation because I am not you. Giving advice might ignore the real problem. In the example above a number of issues have been ignored:

- Is he being bullied by his boss?
- Does he like his work or is he unhappy, and if so, why?
- How does he get on with his colleagues?
- Perhaps there is pressure from home to stay in an unsatisfying job, and this is causing problems in his marriage?
- Does he feel trapped?

- Does he really want to go to college, and what problems would this present?
- Is he clever enough or has he enough motivation to get through a college course? Does he have any doubts about his own abilities?

These are only some of the possible questions ignored by the response, 'The best thing you can do is . . .'. The question for the listener to ask is:

'How can I know what is best for you when I sometimes don't even know what's best for me? In any case, I haven't tried to understand your situation, but simply offered some advice—from my own point of view.'

There is an appropriate time for giving advice, such as when a person needs to fill in an official form, or to see a specialist or other professional such as a solicitor or doctor. The advice

'Go and see a solicitor'

will be viewed in a different way from

'How do you feel about seeking advice from a solicitor?'

One is a direction, the other is a question/suggestion that puts the responsibility for making the decision with the other person.

However, no advice of any kind should be contemplated until the problem has been thoroughly explored. If I do attempt to give you instant advice, I am likely to get it wrong:

'My husband is an alcoholic'.
'The best thing you can do is to leave your husband if he drinks a lot. Look for a place of your own and start a new life. I certainly wouldn't stand for it.'
'But what about the three children?'
'I didn't know you had any children. In that case you'd better stay with him until you know what to do.'
'But he beats me when he's drunk.'

'Well, go and stay with your parents and take the children with you. I know that my parents would help me if my husband behaved like that.'
'But my parents live in a small semi and have only two bedrooms.'
'You could squeeze in until you find somewhere else.'
'The problem is that I have three teenagers, two girls and a boy.'
'That's different, then. You should rent somewhere.'
'But I haven't any money.'
'Then you do have a problem, don't you?'

I cannot begin to give advice, if indeed it is appropriate to give any at all, until I know something about your situation. In any case, what I would do and what is available for me is almost certainly irrelevant for you.

Giving advice *may* be appropriate, but it has always to be based on the other person's needs and resources and on what he or she would like to do.

2 Opinions
We tend not to like what we call 'self-opinionated' people, yet we probably feel flattered when someone asks for our opinion. The problem with giving opinions is that we tend to say:

'Well, if I were you I would . . .'

or

'What I would do is . . .'

The truth is that I can never be you, no matter how sympathetic or empathic I try to be. You sit at the centre of your world, and I sit in mine. Icebergs on the sea of life, we may bump together and even melt a little and join, but I remain separate. My opinions are important, but largely only to me. Even if I am revered by others, the opinions I give are mine based on my experiences of life and not on you or yours.

'If I were you . . .' often means 'If you were me . . .'.

In other words, as with advice, the focus moves away from the person with the problem to the helper or listener. Take this conversation between two women at work:

'I'm thinking of packing in my job here.'
'If I were you I wouldn't do that. There are too few jobs around these days and you might not get another one.'
'I have to pack it in because of my problems with the supervisor.'
'I get on with him all right.'
'Yes, but he doesn't do it to you.'
'I've heard rumours about him, but he's never done anything to me. If I were you I'd just ignore him and he'll stop it.'
'But you don't have to work with him as closely as I do.'
'No, but I know him well and don't think he really means anything by it. Maybe he's just trying to be friendly and you misunderstand what's happening? If he really is doing it then what I would do is ask him to stop it and tell him to leave me alone. If he didn't, I would report him to someone.'
'But you don't know what it's like. He does it most of the time and I can't think of what to do. I can't get away from him.'
'Are you sure you aren't imagining it?'

The problem again is that the listener hasn't really listened and she constantly moves the focus back to herself. She hasn't even established what it is the supervisor does to this other woman. Consider this totally different approach:

'I'm thinking of packing in my job here.'
'You seem to be very agitated and upset about something.'
'Well, it's my supervisor.'
'So, something about your supervisor you find distressing?'

'Well, he won't leave me alone—I mean physically.'
'So you object very strongly to something he does to you?'
'Yes, he . . .'

Here the listener does not offer an opinion, but reflects what the other person is saying. Hopefully, the use of this and other listening skills will enable them both to work through the problem in a more understanding and helpful way.

3 Sympathy
Sympathy can be very supportive and comforting:

'I am sorry to hear about your husband. It must be awful for you.'

But it might be offered as:

'I feel really sorry for you. The same thing happened to me so I know how you feel and what you are going through.'

Even if we have had similar experiences, it is never the *same*, because we are different people and will react in different ways. If I have lost a baby at three months and you have a similar experience, I must not imagine, even if I have some feelings that are similar to yours, that I necessarily know what you are feeling or experiencing. The same applies to all experiences of life, both good and bad. At its worst, sympathy can be expressed as:

'You are getting divorced? Well, I've been divorced three times and you think you've got problems—you should hear what happened to me.'

In other words:

'I know how you feel—but my experience was much worse.'

And if I am, in fact, still working through my own problems I will probably be so tied up in my own feelings that I am the last person to be able to help. Often, the best helpers are those who have progressed through their own suffering and come to some kind of healing and acceptance. Such people are unlikely to say, 'I know how you feel.'

4   Practical help
This is the typically 'British' way:

> 'Don't just stand there and say how sorry you are. *Do* something.'

But this response can bring with it the same problems as above. Giving practical help can be very constructive, but it may prevent the troubled person from realising what she is facing or feeling:

> 'The baby is getting me down, and I don't think I can cope.'
> 'Have the afternoon off and get some rest. I'll look after the baby for you. Don't worry, I can manage.'

Very practical and sensible—but is it always helpful? It may well provide a needed rest or stop-gap, but it could be missing the point:

- What is causing the depression?
- Are there problems at home or at work?
- Perhaps she has an alcoholic husband?
- Maybe there are problems with the baby at home?
- Could it be postnatal depression?
- Is there a financial or a marital problem?
- Is she frightened she might hurt the baby?

Also, if I say, 'I can manage', this might make her feel worse—more inadequate and, therefore, more depressed.

Practical help is often good as a temporary expedient, but it may not help the person on the receiving end to examine her problems or to move towards a possible solution, unless it gives her the time to go to a good listener or counsellor.

*   *   *

However, although giving advice, opinions, sympathy or practical help are four ways in which we may well respond to others who come to us for help, they might all miss the real point. They move the focus of the problem from *you*, the speaker with the problems, to *me*, the listener. If we are really to help we need to help others to look at the roots of the problems in their own world and in their own way:

> 'I feel terrible and I don't know what to do. My wife has just run off with another man and I feel dreadful.'
> 'Gosh, that's awful. I know how you feel, though. I've had a rough day myself, what with the slump in the stock market and the recession.'

In other words, 'I am not really interested in you and your day and haven't even listened to what you have said.'

Take another example:

> 'I don't seem to be able to cope very well with my work.'

Unhelpful responses:

> 'Well, I've felt like that a number of times. You've just got to get on with it. That's what I did.'
> 'If I were you I'd just carry on until things become easier.'
> 'You've had this before, so perhaps you're in the wrong job.'
> 'You look awful. What you should do is have a few days off sick.'
> 'I am sorry about this—and I know, because I've been there myself.'
> 'You've coped before, so there must be something wrong with you.'

Helpful responses:

> 'So you're finding things difficult.'
> 'It seems as though things are not easy for you at present.'

'In what ways do you find it difficult to cope?'
'What things do you find difficult?'

Here the listener is really listening; his responses show that he cares, and he is not being judgemental or focusing the problem back on to himself. He is not giving advice, not expressing an opinion, not saying he is sorry and not immediately offering to do something for the person in trouble. Together with the other skills of listening to be outlined later, this approach can help the other person to begin the process of self-exploration so that she can come to a better understanding of her predicament and then, hopefully, be better able to decide what to do about it.

It is worth remembering that there are no magic-wand solutions. The statement 'I've lost my job' might mean:

'I can easily get another one.'
'I will be out of work for months—perhaps years.'
'I can no longer pay my mortgage.'
'I will have to sell my car and move house.'
'I feel devastated and rejected.'

Whichever of these is nearest to the truth, the statement may hide feelings of despair, anger, failure, relief or sadness—and all or any of these are important to the speaker.

The basis of this kind of listening is that the helper keeps the focus on the other person, encouraging her to work through her problems and feelings in her own way and, as far as is possible, by using her own resources.

THE THREE-STAGE APPROACH

One method of helping, often used in counselling, is based on the three-stage model of Gerard Egan.[3] It is a useful model for all listeners and helpers. The three stages are

---

[3]   Egan, G. *The Skilled Helper*, Monterey, Calif: Brooks Cole, 1975.

exploration, understanding and action. At the most basic level, this is how the individual with the problem should be encouraged to perceive these stages:

1 The present: I will look at what is happening in my life now and *explore* this as widely as possible.
2 The past: I will then look at why the problems have arisen and where they have come from, and what and who the contributing factors are. This should help me to *understand* the situation better.
3 The future: Finally, I will look at what possible avenues there are for me and try to make choices and take *action*.

1 Exploration

In this first stage the listener focuses her complete attention on the other person, and uses the basic skills of listening and responding—prompting, mirroring, paraphrasing, reflecting, summarising and asking questions. (We look at these in Chapter 10.) In line with Carl Rogers, the listener offers genuineness, acceptance and empathy, without criticising or seeking solutions.

> When I asked one of my clients what she thought of what we were doing, she said that she thought of me as a 'big listening ear'.

This listening ear then encourages the individual with the problem to explore his own world. It is rather like opening a new book half-way through chapter 6, and then going back to the beginning of the chapter in order to take in the whole of that chapter; next, discovering that some of the pages are stuck together and cannot yet be torn apart; so then looking back at the earlier chapters. Simply put, it is a matter of getting the other person to tell his own story as far as he is able and, by using the skills of listening, of helping him to uncover more and more detail, not just of the story, but also of the emotions that lie in and behind it. In other words, *you*, the listener, help *him* to examine *his* world, as far as is possible, thereby starting the long process that can lead to some kind of understanding. You need to exercise great sensitivity in the way you respond, because your client may be embarrassed, upset, nervous or anxious.

In this first stage there is often a focus on the 'facts' as perceived by the other person, although some emotions may emerge. She wishes to tell you the story, from *her* point of view—and you must take this into account, especially when dealing with relationship problems:

> A smart and tidy little woman comes to see you. 'My husband is an animal'—and she then tells you a story to melt your heart about this horrible man she lives with. You feel angry about this monster who bullies her and dominates her life. When he comes to see you later, you are expecting a heavyweight thug, but are faced with a mild-mannered little man who looks as though he wouldn't hurt a fly and who tells you about this 'old cow' he lives with. If he had come to see you first, you might have ended up with an image of a shrew of a wife. The problem is that the 'facts' related by each of them are from the same situation. They are both telling the 'truth' as they see and feel it.

The task here would be to help them both to explore their own world rather than just focus on what they see as the faults of their partner, and to try to create some kind of understanding about what is happening in the relationship now.

This exploration stage should be taken gently, so that the client is led from perceived facts to feelings. To say, 'My husband is an animal' tells a great deal about feelings and leaves you, the listener, in no doubt about the way she perceives both him and his behaviour. Such statements should never be ignored or thought of as just angry or hurt ramblings. They must be explored. But you should never agree with such statements—you must not say:

> 'I see what you mean. He must be a pig to behave like that.'

For the client may respond in a very defensive manner:

'Don't you talk about my husband like that! What do you know of him, anyway?'

In other words, sometimes people feel that they can say things about their partner, or their world, that others should not.

On the other hand, if the client responds positively to the listener's negative comment, then the listener moves into a collusive partnership where he or she is seen as being 'on my side' against the other person. By giving an opinion and making a judgement you, the listener, have moved the focus back on to yourself and may have made the client defensive. By showing her that you agree with her, you have slipped into one of the more hazardous ways of trying to be sympathetic. This can be equally true of situations at work, where two people are in disagreement. There as elsewhere, the listener/helper should not take sides, except where a mistake has been made, or someone is definitely in the wrong, or has broken the rules or procedures. But even then, any listener needs first to listen to all sides of the story. This stage of exploration should concentrate on establishing an open relationship with the person who has the problem, so that he or she begins, however slowly, to learn to trust you and feel that you are not sitting in judgement, either on him or her or on anyone else.

When people come with problems, they usually have three things on their minds:

1   They want to sort out the *confusion*.
2   They want to be able to see what *choices* are available to them.
3   They want to discover where and how they can make *changes* in their lives.

By developing a relationship of trust, working through these three phases, the listener enables the client to look as widely as possible at his or her problems. As the client talks and explores, he or she will begin to reveal specific problem areas:

> John and Kathleen came for help, saying that their marriage was breaking down and they didn't know what to do. John was smartly dressed but looked angry and confused. Kathleen was dressed in black from head to toe and was very weepy, looking just as though she had come from a funeral. They had been married for twenty years and their daughter was just leaving home to go to university. They had lived almost separate lives since their marriage, partly because of his work. Kathleen thought that she was not very bright, but that John was intelligent and successful—which he was. While they talked, he implied that he had come only because she had 'nagged' him about it. When asked about their family, Kathleen said that they had one daughter, but added that a baby boy had been born who had died at three months almost twenty years ago. They said they had coped with it, but the fact that Kathleen was dressed as if in mourning and that he was resentful made me think that perhaps this needed to be explored. When asked about the death of the baby, they eventually said that they had never been allowed to talk about it, either between themselves or with anyone else. Kathleen had become pregnant before they married and they had lived with her mother. It was her mother who had forbidden them to talk about it. Also, John came from a background where men did not cry and had to be firmly in charge of themselves and their families. Kathleen, in fact, was a bright girl but had never measured up to her parents' expectations. She had been successful at school, but it had not been enough and her parents always said that she should and could have done better. This was the pattern of their behaviour towards her, and her 'having to get married' was the last blow. When the baby died, her mother told her to put it behind her and never to mention it again.

A number of pointers began to emerge:

- The crisis point was the daughter leaving home, for the two of them would then be on their own together for the first time.

- They had vivid memories of the death of the baby— something they had never faced or talked about.
- Both were grieving inwardly and needed to talk about it.
- Both had difficult backgrounds and had learned strategies for coping, but these were inappropriate for the problems in their relationship. She had a low self-esteem and he felt compelled to try to be strong because he was a man.

These were only some of the problems they had to be encouraged to explore together. They had to be helped to bring these events, and the feelings surrounding and emanating from them, out into the open so that, hopefully, they would be able to grasp what the feelings were, where they came from, and what they were doing to their relationship.

In the workplace, such a case would be more likely to come to the attention of a welfare officer or occupational health nurse than to that of a manager or supervisor, and would probably concern only one person in the relationship. The example of John and Kathleen shows how important initial impressions are, and we need to ask what these tell us about people and about their problems.

So this first stage, exploration, helps both them and you to look at their world. It is rather like being in a minefield: you have to tread carefully. But the mines have to be found and exposed and, if possible, defused or detonated— but only in conditions of safety and with the help of an individual trained in the appropriate skills. For the person with the problem, it is a question of looking at the present and the presenting problems and examining them as widely as possible. 'Lateral thinking' can be useful here. What this means is that you look at as many nooks and crannies as possible and explore all the avenues that gradually open up. You do this by listening to your client's statement and the meaning within it, and then questioning him as widely as you can about the possible implications. This will be looked at later when we consider the skills of listening, of asking questions and of looking at solutions and goals.

2 Understanding

In this second stage of Gerard Egan's approach the emphasis is on helping the client to look deeper into the iceberg that is herself. She should also begin to be able to see her problems in a new light and from a different perspective:

> 'The penny begins to drop and a glimmer of light begins to dawn.'
> 'I can see things more clearly now, and am beginning to understand how and why they happened and why I react as I do.'

The listener's task now is to show deeper empathy—it is rather like listening to a piece of music and being able to pick out the bass and alto lines rather than just the tune or melody. Going back to the idea of the iceberg and the hidden agenda, we are trying to allow the experiences and feelings from below the surface to emerge. Consciously your client may be completely unaware of these, but careful questioning in a safe and accepting environment can lead to a new realisation and self-discovery. It may also lead to feelings of shame, anger, guilt or resentment, or to denial. Sometimes the task is to look for things that are not said, or to pay more attention to expressions that don't seem to fit or are too glib. For example, what do the inconsistencies in this story mean?

> Elizabeth came for help and said at one stage, 'I have a wonderful, supportive mother. In fact, she's the best mother in the world. She brought us up to respect others. Mind you, she still criticises me like she did when we were young.' This eventually led to her saying, 'The other day I came downstairs wearing a new dress and she asked me why I was wearing something that was too young for me. And she said that the shoes didn't match, either. But she's a really wonderful mother and I love her very much.' Elizabeth was thirty-eight years old, married, had three children and was having problems in her marriage to Brian,

a teacher. She came for help initially because she just couldn't cope with the criticisms that she received from him. But how could she say that she had a wonderful mother when her mother had done (and was still doing) to her exactly what Brian was doing? How could she say, 'I love her very much', when she had to endure more and more criticism of almost everything she said or did? It took a long time for Elizabeth to eventually scream, 'I hate her, I hate her, the bitch.' The 'truth' was hidden deep in the iceberg, defended by feelings she thought she *ought* to have for her mother. Her ambivalent feelings came out in her remarks and needed to be explored in order to create some understanding.

Experience may lead us to be suspicious of anyone who says they have a wonderful mother, husband, father, partner, children, job—or anything else.

Part of this second stage, of creating understanding, is to look for any possible external help and resources. Give any information that you can about avenues open to your client, about who and what may be able to help. She will be reassured to know that there are people and agencies available to give assistance. A person facing problems in her early fifties may need to know about the menopause or about the possible effects of children growing up and leaving home—both major stages in life. For some people there may be fears of illness, anxieties about a new baby in the family, about an abortion or being unemployed or made redundant; about moving house, children experimenting with drugs, divorce, debt, alcoholism, retirement or bereavement. In all these cases, to be able to give information can help to create understanding.

This second stage should lead to progress in the search not only for what can be done generally, but for what the client can do for herself. From an exploration of present problems (Stage 1) we have moved to an attempt to understand where those problems have come from and how they are influencing the present (Stage 2).

3 Action

The third stage in this listening and helping process is about concentration on decision-making and attempting to find solutions. Possible new methods of coping can be examined and even learned, and a plan of action worked out. The person with the problem can be helped to look at what is possible for him—at what he can do—and what the consequences might be for him and for those around him. A useful start is to make a list of possible avenues or solutions and to consider how these might affect all those involved.

When I have a problem and am looking for solutions I have to think of what I would like to do, but I must also look closely at what is possible for me. I cannot choose what is impossible. For example, if my marriage is breaking down I might write a list of five possible choices:

1   to go to a solicitor and seek advice about separation and divorce;
2   to stay together for the sake of the children and for financial reasons;
3   to do nothing and allow the situation to continue;
4   to take steps to put the relationship right, such as going to Relate for counselling;
5   to leave my partner and home and find a new life.

There are, of course, other possibilities such as burning the house down, suicide or murder, but these would hardly be acceptable options.

Most of all I would like to put the marriage right (4), although staying together for whatever reasons (2) would be acceptable to me as second best. I could not endure doing nothing (3), and do not wish to leave home (5)—at least, not yet. It may be that my decisions and whatever solutions I choose are already limited or decided for me. My wife may have been to see a solicitor and be determined on a divorce; will not consider anything else or change her mind, and will not go with me to Relate for marital counselling. I could choose to go on my own, but believe that without my partner present this would not be helpful.

So what I would like is tempered by what is possible and by the decisions, needs and choices of others, and I have to face this and try to come to terms with the situation. I could still choose to go to Relate on my own, see a solicitor, and leave home and find a place of my own. But any of these could create or leave me with a number of other problems—not least, feelings of anger or guilt. They could also create further financial difficulties for everyone, to say nothing of the effect on the children.

These three stages—exploration, understanding and action—are not separate and distinct activities. The listener applies the same skills of listening and questioning throughout, but the interreactions between her and her client should gradually become deeper and wider. Initially the person with the problem is helped to explore his world through the empathy and acceptance of the listener, whose listening and responding skills involve working from the top of the human iceberg, then probing deeper under the surface so that hidden thoughts, emotions and experiences begin to emerge. The individual is helped to explore as many areas of his present life as possible, and this should enable him to look at himself in a new light. The listener uses further skills that challenge the assumptions, beliefs and ideas that have been put forward, and attempts to put into context anything expressed that does not seem to fit in with the rest of the story. She is helping her client to probe the past as well as the present, in order to see where the problems have come from. In the third stage, the concern is to look at what possibilities for change are available and what decisions can be made. The client should ultimately feel that he knows what he can or cannot do and, hopefully, should be able to accept what the possibilities for him are.

There is often no simple solution to our problems, but we *can* be helped to face them and to manage them in a more effective manner. If your husband dies, the only useful and effective option, other than trying to keep a stiff upper lip, is to accept that this is an extremely painful experience that cannot be ignored. You either try to get over it through denial, get stuck in the middle and find that you cannot move forward, or you move through the experience to healing and renewal.

Sometimes the problems that emerge are so painful that the person experiencing them may walk away from both the problems and the helper. But to choose not to be helped, however much the potential helper may regret it, is one of the options open to all.

9 Learning to Listen

We all like to think that we are good listeners, and we don't care much for people who don't listen to us when we speak.

Imagine that you are at a party talking to someone. This person doesn't look directly at you, but keeps glancing around the room and saying, 'Ummm. Ah–ah. Yeah. Ummm'. His face is vacant, and the message coming across to you strongly is: 'I'm not listening to you.' Perhaps he is bored with you, or is he looking for someone more important to talk to?

The point is, we can usually tell when a person isn't listening to us. It even shows in the way he stands or sits. One method of dealing with a non-listener when you are talking to him is to stop talking and wait for his response. Usually there is a short silence and then he says something like, 'Oh, sorry. What were you saying?' He may then make some insignificant comment and move away. Or you could stop talking and move on, and he will probably hardly be aware that someone was talking to him.

There is an old saying that we have two ears and one mouth, so we should listen twice as much as we speak. But it often tends to be the other way around. As a famous golfer said of a rival, 'His ears are brand new, but his mouth is worn out!' When the infamous Lord Byron's tempestuous relationship with Lady Caroline Lamb cooled down he is supposed to have said, 'She has lost the power of communication, but not, regrettably, the gift of speech!' Unfortunately, when we are talking too much and not really listening, others soon pick up the signals.

In facing other people we present who and what we are, and everything about us speaks to them—physically, verbally, emotionally and psychologically. If I am failing to listen properly, my face may show a complete lack of interest *or* it may be screwed up with concern. I may stand close to the person and touch her arm, *or* keep my distance. I can say anything from 'Um', 'Oh' or 'Fancy that' to 'Tell me more' or 'That must have been awful. What happened next?'. All the time, my own thoughts and feelings may remain locked away and hidden—*or* I may express them by crying or by laughing out loud.

ARE WE REALLY LISTENING?

There are a number of other ways in which, even unconsciously, we signal that we are not listening, or show that our thoughts are elsewhere:

1   *Ignoring*

You can completely ignore what the other person is saying, while pretending to be listening. You have the right look on your face and the correct bodily attitude, but you are not listening. Or you may simply be thinking of something else, such as what you are going to do that evening, or whether you remembered to lock your car when you parked it. Or you might even totally change direction by suddenly asking an irrelevant question or by raising another issue:

> 'We had a terrible row and then my husband said he was leaving me.'
> 'Oh! And where did you both go for your holidays last year?'

2   *Comparing*

As already mentioned, we may compare what the other person says with our own experiences or with those of others. We may do this silently and internally or by stating it baldly:

'That's not as serious as Mrs Brown's problems.'

This involves a dismissive attitude on the part of the listener—here we are taking it upon ourselves to decide what is and what is not important. Comparing in this case, in this way, is not likely to be helpful for either the listener or the speaker because it moves the focus elsewhere—to Mrs Brown—and is almost certainly irrelevant.

3 Judging and criticising

This is similar to expressing the sort of opinion that tells the other person what you would or would not do if you were in her shoes:

'You're stupid if you do that.'
'Why on earth did you do that? It's only made matters worse.'
'I wouldn't do that.'
'Why didn't you . . .?'

Here again, the focus moves back to you, the listener: you are making judgements about what the other person has done or intends doing. You may also be criticising her actions without discovering exactly what she has done or will do, and why. Even if you do know why, it is generally unhelpful to criticise what the other person might have done or might decide to do. Her likely reaction is to feel insulted or humiliated. Also, when the listener, as here, is sitting above the other person like a judge, this may make her feel belittled and angry.

4 Advising

Again we come to advice. It has already been argued that this is unhelpful when it comes across as:

'What I think you should do is . . .'

'The best thing you can do is . . .'

Once more it places the focus on the listener and not on the client.

5   *Agreeing*
You can decide to agree with whatever is said:

'You were right to do that.'
'Your boss must be awful to have done that.'

But this establishes a collusion with the other person, who may now believe that you are simply there to go along with whatever she says or does. You stop being a helper, and become a partner with her in whatever she may do. At this point she will cease to explore her situation and thus also cease, together with the listener, to make progress in understanding the problem.

6   *Thinking ahead*
Often this takes the form of working out what you are going to say next, and moves the focus very firmly from the speaker to the listener. Thinking ahead is necessary, but must be based on what the client has said.

All of these barriers against listening give a clear message of rejection. What we do, what we say and how we react will shout out either:

'I'm listening and interested in you'

or

'Go away. I don't want to know.'

One problem is that of *confrontation*. Take the following meeting between a parent and a teacher at a large school:

Parent: I've come to see you about Darren. He's in your class and I'm very unhappy about the way he is being taught.

Teacher: Well, I am sorry, but the new system has to be followed whether you like it or not. We've all got to get used to new methods and ideas.

Parent: Look, I might be old-fashioned, but I think that the old methods were better and everything now seems so vague and pointless.

Teacher: What do you mean, vague and pointless? I've been a teacher for twenty years and I know my job. It might seem pointless to you, but I know what it's all about, even if I'm not totally happy with it either.

Parent: I suppose you mean well, but just look at Darren. He's dropped back almost to the bottom of the class since the new methods were introduced.

Teacher: Well, he's not the brightest boy in the world, is he?

Parent: Not the brightest? What do you mean by that? He's not thick, if that's what you mean. In any case, it's your job to get the best out of him. That's what teachers are for, isn't it? Mind you, all you teachers are alike these days. You're not interested in those who aren't very clever. It's all to do with comparing one school with another in the league tables, isn't it? It's not good for the school if you don't get good exam results, so you concentrate on the bright ones.

Teacher: That's nonsense. We do our best for everyone here and we haven't always got what we want. There's a shortage of money, books, paper and other things we need. We don't have the time to do everything.

Parent: I'm not interested in your problems, I'm concerned about Darren. What are you going to do to help him, or are you just saying that you can't be bothered?

Teacher: Don't get shirty with me, Mrs Jones. Of course I'm bothered. In any case, you can't tell me my job. I've been a teacher too long for that.

Parent: (shouting) I'm not telling you your job, I just want Darren to get on better. We had the same problems with his previous teacher. He didn't care and neither do you.

Teacher: (angry) Well, I'm sorry you're not satisfied, but it's no good getting angry with me, and what his other teacher was like is nothing to do with me. It's not my fault. I suggest that you see the head if you have any complaints . . .

The parent, angry and upset, demands that her son should have the best help possible. She is aggressive almost from the start, and ready for battle. Obviously she is very worried about her son and is criticising the new system as well as the teachers. The teacher, on the defensive, retreats behind his professional role. Nobody can tell him his job. He directs the blame at other areas such as shortage of money and equipment, and feels that he is being 'got at' for something that isn't his fault. His final gesture of exasperation is to point Mrs Jones to the head teacher.

A similar confrontation could take place in an office:

Clerk: I'm having problems with this new machine and finding it difficult to cope.

Supervisor: What do you mean, problems? I managed all right.

Clerk: It's hard, not like the old machine. I know you showed me how to use it, but I don't find it easy.

Supervisor: You can't blame me for your mistakes. I can use it without any problems.

Clerk: I'm not blaming you, but you've been on a course.

Supervisor: I know, but I've told you what to do and you'll just have to get used to it.

Clerk: I suppose I'm old-fashioned, but I don't like new-fangled things and changes.

Supervisor: We've all got to get used to change. It's no use living in the past. This machine means that your work will be more efficient.

Clerk: What do you mean, more efficient? I coped with the old one and got on with my work well enough. Are you saying that I wasn't working hard enough before this machine came along?

Supervisor: We brought in the machines to update our system, and to make things easier and better.

Clerk: I don't find it better. I keep making mistakes and having to start all over again. That doesn't get things done quicker.

Supervisor: Well, you'll just have to work harder at it. I don't find it difficult, so I can't see what the problem is for you.

Clerk: The problem is that you're not being very helpful, are you?

Supervisor: I can't help it if you can't cope with the work.

Clerk: Can't cope! It's not me, it's this ****** machine.

Supervisor: There's no need to swear at me just because you can't handle things.

Clerk: I wasn't swearing at you, and I could cope if you'd take the time to show me what to do instead of getting on your high horse.

Supervisor: Look, I'm the supervisor around here and you'll just get on with it and do as you are told. Stop complaining.

The confrontation gradually builds up, and the supervisor makes no attempt to stop it by helping the clerk or by asking what the problems are. Not a very good supervisor and not a good system, when a member of staff is so poorly prepared for using new equipment.

Before we look at the specific skills involved in listening, we need to consider two other factors, both of which contribute to good or poor listening: the environment and body language.

THE ENVIRONMENT

One day at work someone comes up to you and asks if he can have a word with you. This could happen on the shop floor, in a factory, in the office, canteen or corridor, or in any other part of the workplace. You now have to decide whether to say, 'Go ahead' on the spot, or whether to go somewhere private. If you have an office, you could say, 'Let's go to my office and we can talk in private.' You will need to ask this person which he prefers, and he may just say, 'Oh, we can talk here. I don't mind.'

The room
Where the session is held is important.

- Is it an office, surgery, study or consulting room?
- What does the room/place look like?
- Is it comfortable, and does it give the impression of efficiency?
- Is it rather scruffy with uncomfortable furniture?
- Are there overflowing ashtrays and a general air of untidiness and disorganisation?
- Is there a desk, and do you sit behind it?
- Is there a window or bright light behind you so that the other person cannot see your face?
- Is your chair more comfortable, larger and higher than his or hers?

- May the telephone ring, or is the answering-machine likely to switch on at any time?
- May someone walk into the room for some reason?
- Can people look into the room from the outside and see who is there?

Any of the possibilities listed here can be threatening to someone who is worried, nervous or depressed. Certain pictures, posters, even furniture—and certainly the state of the room—may cause anger or unease in someone in trouble. So if we are to create the right environment for listening, there are certain positive things that we can do, and negative aspects that we can guard against.

If it is a room that is to be the venue for the meeting, it should be well laid out and equipped with decent, comfortable furniture, and the whole effect should create a feeling of ease. There could be bookshelves and cabinets, a desk covered with letters, papers and files and a telephone and an answering and Fax machine. All this could suggest someone who is probably pretty busy, but who has time enough to listen. This room, probably an office, should indicate that a professional approach is being taken yet be comfortable enough for people to be able to relax. It should preferably be decorated in pastel shades, and there should be curtains or venetian blinds at the windows so that others cannot look in.

Desks and chairs

The chairs should be comfortable, but not huge and plush so that you almost disappear into them and feel distanced from the other person. They should be of the same type and size: to sit in a higher chair than the other person gives the impression that you are or think you are more important and provides you with a distinct psychological advantage, so that he may feel that he is at a psychological disadvantage. If there is a desk, there should also be an area where you can sit informally. Sitting behind a desk gives an air of authority and distance which is not conducive to either good listening or good talking. The chairs should not directly face each other, but be placed at a slight angle, so that if there are two of you you are not in a confrontational position. To sit directly opposite someone who is already feeling anxious or embarrassed can make him feel even more uneasy. Having the chairs at a slight angle gives a psychological and physical 'escape route'. Do not have more chairs than people—an empty chair can be very threatening, especially when there is a third party involved who is not present. The third chair can easily represent them and cause severe discomfort. However, in counselling, empty chairs can be used effectively to simulate the presence of another person. An empty chair can speak volumes about someone who isn't there, giving that person a presence and a reality.

> Carol was having problems with Paula, a colleague at work who always seemed to be criticising her. When she went to see her supervisor about it, she found that an empty chair formed a triangle with her's and the supervisor's. Carol became increasingly aware of the chair, feeling that it represented Paula. She became upset, and felt very threatened until the supervisor removed it.

Similarly, if you place a third chair when there are only two of you present, it is useful to ask questions such as:

'How does it feel having another chair there?'
'How would you feel if the person who is persecuting you at work were sitting there in that chair? What would you say to her if you could?'

So chairs can be powerful tools in looking at what is happening in a relationship and how the troubled person feels about it.

The chairs should not be so far apart as to be distancing and not so close as to be threatening. Having them too close could prevent the other person from talking and feeling at

ease. You, the listener, should sit relaxed and upright, but
not too stiff or with folded arms. If possible, place a small
coffee table in between and in front of the chairs, forming a
triangle. This helps to create an atmosphere of informality
and ease. You could also have a vase of flowers on the table,
a box of tissues and, if appropriate, an ashtray. If you or the
client are a smoker, come to some arrangement about this at
the beginning of the session.

Avoiding interruptions

Either the telephone should be unplugged or calls should be
transferred to another extension. There should also be a
large 'Do not enter' or 'Do not disturb' notice on the door.
Make sure there is no clear glass in the door or between
offices, in case others are able to see who is there. If
someone suddenly comes into the room or peers through a
glass partition or the telephone rings when the individual is
telling you about his problem, it may destroy any feeling of
confidence or confidentiality:

> Barbara was having difficulty at work with a colleague and
> asked to see the supervisor. She was taken to an office
> where she slowly began to talk about the problem. She was
> embarrassed and anxious and did not want any of her
> colleagues to know about it. Suddenly the door opened and
> a clerk entered, saying, 'I've just got to get something from
> that cupboard.' Barbara was so upset that she got up and left
> the office immediately, leaving the supervisor and the clerk
> not knowing what to do.

Time and timing

There are situations where you, the listener, need to offer as
much time as the person in trouble needs. It would be
unhelpful if you said to someone who came to see you
whose wife had died recently, 'Well, I've got an hour and
then I have to go.' However limited your time, in such an
instance it would be better to offer an open-ended session at
some other mutually acceptable time. And the way you put

it matters a lot. You must never give the impression that others are imposing on your precious time—for instance, by responding with:

> 'Well [looking at watch], I suppose I can spare you half an hour.'
> 'I'm rather busy, but I might be able to fit you in.'
> 'I have a lot on my plate at the moment, but I might be able to give you a few minutes of my time later today.'

But offering people unlimited time can create problems— 'When you are to be hanged tomorrow it concentrates the mind wonderfully.' There is some truth in this and, applied to our situation, it might prevent a person from just rambling on. It is also good planning to think in terms of time 'allocated' rather than 'limited' for listening sessions. Again, it depends on how you say it—'I've only an hour' is rather different from 'We can have an hour together this morning.'

Other positive responses:

> 'Certainly you can come and talk to me. I've an hour free this afternoon if that's convenient for you. Can you come at two o'clock?'
> 'How about this morning from ten until eleven, and if we need more time we can make another appointment for tomorrow, if you wish.'

An hour is actually a long time for someone to talk and the other to listen effectively: it takes a great deal of physical energy and mental concentration. To have more than an hour could mean that you, the listener, begin to switch off, and you might even become bored with the story, especially if your listening skills are poor. If an hour is not long enough, another appointment can be made for later.

It is also a good idea to have a large clock in the room, in such a position that you can see it without moving your eyes too much. Or you might use a small movable clock that you could place on a shelf or cabinet, or on the wall behind the speaker and slightly to one side.

Then, there will be times when it is just not convenient to see someone, for whatever reason. Making an appointment for a definite time and place confirms that you are busy, but that you are making time for him or her.

Getting the place right is important, for it can give out signals that put people at ease, give them confidence and trust both in you and in themselves, and enable them to talk freely.

BODY LANGUAGE

It is important to look at the other person:

- What kind of state is she in?
- How does she look and react?
- Is she relaxed and at ease, does she seem anxious and agitated?
- Does she seem to be sad or depressed?
- Are her shoulders hunched?
- Does she look you in the eye or does she avoid eye contact?
- How does she walk?
- How is she dressed?

Does she sit on the edge of the chair and clutch her handbag tightly? At what point does she take out her cigarettes? Does she rub her hands together nervously or clasp them so that her knuckles show white?

All of these can tell you something about her state of mind before you begin to listen. If you are in an office, you may be able to offer her tea or coffee, which may help her to relax and give her time to compose herself. You need to be sensitive enough to read the messages coming across from her, even before she speaks, and then try to help her to feel at ease with you.

What about *your* posture? You can ask the same questions of yourself as about the other person, for her initial reaction to you will be determined by what she sees of you:

- What kind of a state are you in, and how do you look and react?
- However you are feeling, does it show?
- Are you very busy, and aware of it and showing it?
- What does she think of you, and what is the relationship between you?
- Are you her supervisor or manager, and how does this affect the relationship?

Do not lounge back in your chair—sit upright but make yourself comfortable. This tells the other person that you are alert and ready to listen, but relaxed. Some books on body language tell you not to cross your legs because this can be seen as a 'defensive gesture'; but most people sit with their legs crossed and this is acceptable, as long as you don't swing one leg up and down all the time—this may sound an odd caution, but a surprising number of people do it.

Expression

Eyes   Do not stare at people—look at them. When we are talking to someone we usually adopt a particular strategy— almost unconsciously. To begin with, we establish eye contact by looking firmly at the person. Partly because we believe it is rude to stare at people, but also because it can be embarrassing, we glance away for a few seconds. We then look back at him to see if he is still listening and looking at us, and then we glance away again. We do this throughout the time we are speaking and then, when we get to the end of what we are saying, we usually establish firm eye contact again. This final eye contact checks whether or not the other person is listening, and says, 'What I have been saying to you is important, isn't it?'

So you, the listener, should neither stare nor be looking away most of the time. You might look at his eyes and then slightly alter your gaze to look at the rest of his face or shoulders. But it would not be helpful to be looking at his shoulders when he is looking at you.

Try to look concerned. Don't squint with concentration, *or* let your eyes go blank with lack of interest. If you wear spectacles, can you see without them? They might act as a barrier between the two of you, especially dark glasses or the half-glasses used for reading that you have to peer over. Do not raise your eyebrows or furrow them, unless in an expression that is slightly questioning yet accepting.

Observing the way *he* looks or glances away can tell you something about him and how he feels:

- Does he avoid eye contact completely?
- Is this because he is shy or feeling embarrassed and upset, or is he telling lies?

Staring can indicate excitement, or shock and numbness.

Mouth Do not pout or narrow your lips unless this is part of showing that you are interested and listening to the story.

Nose Do not screw up your nose or sniff constantly. Be careful about blowing your nose as this can be a distraction and might suggest that you are not listening.

The impression you should give is of someone who is at ease but who is concerned about this other person and interested in what he or she has to say. Hopefully this is not just an impression, but a reality. You are not posing or acting a part, but genuinely showing that you are listening and want to help in whatever way you can.

Gestures

Use what are called 'open' arm and leg gestures. This means, for instance, not folding your arms or sitting hunched up in your chair with your head down. Do not scratch, pick, fidget, yawn or keep stretching your legs and body. You can put your arms and hands at waist level with your palms facing slightly outwards and upwards, and this will say to the other person:

'Here I am. I am ready to listen. Talk to me.'

Open gestures are postures and movements that show the other person that you are receptive to her and that you accept her.

Be aware, also, of *her* gestures and movements:

- If you shook hands, was she uneasy about shaking hands with you?
- Is she indicating that she doesn't want to come too close to you?
- How is she sitting and moving?
- Does she look as though she doesn't want to be there, even as if she could just crawl away and die?
- Does she look as though she is looking for comfort and sympathy?
- Is she sitting bolt upright with her body all tense and stiff?

While you listen, don't sit completely still, and don't constantly shift around in your chair, either. Nod when appropriate, and with a genuine look of concern on your face. You need to move, even if only to show that you are still alive, but make your movements slow and deliberate. Once you are in a comfortable position you may not need to move much.

Body space
We usually do not like to be too close to someone we don't know, and in order to protect ourselves and feel comfortable we have our own body space. In other words, we have rules about how close we allow others to get to us. There are four main categories of body space:

1 *Intimate* The area is strictly reserved for close family—for partner, lover and children. It involves such things as holding hands and putting an arm around some-one—gestures implying that these people are close. The closeness is not only physical, but psychological. The first

intimacy of this kind is between a baby and his mother, with holding and cuddling, skin-to-skin contact and feeding at the breast. This activity produces what is usually called 'bonding'. For adults, the ultimate may be sexual contact, but it also involves hugging and kissing.

2 *Personal* The space that we reserve for others as the circle begins to widen—for other members of the family and close friends, and perhaps for a few that we are close to at work.

3 *Social* The space that is generally for colleagues at work, for people at parties and for social occasions where it is sometimes difficult to avoid being close to each other. But we still do not like to be too close, although at events like football matches people are often content to be close to others even if they have no choice, and may even speak to complete strangers.

4 *Public* The space that we allow for everyone else in the world. Note how we behave on public transport. If you travel on the London Underground notice where two or three people sit when they enter an empty carriage. If they know each other they sit together. If not, they sit apart and leave gaps between each other. If someone comes into a carriage where there are others, he may even sit as far away from them as possible. Note also what happens on the Underground when the train stops between stations. Usually no one speaks, no matter how crowded it is. People who attend church regularly usually sit in the same seats every week and can be very put out if they find someone else sitting there. The same applies to some local pubs, where certain people have their own seats, sometimes even marked with their name. Think also how people behave on holiday abroad. They tend to mark out their territory and expect to have it the next day, even if it means laying out their towels early in the morning when they are not going to be there for some hours.

Observing the body-language rules also means that you should not, by the position that you take up, bar a person's way—there should be an 'escape route' for him. Chairs should be at an angle and at what is a comfortable distance for both parties, depending on their relationship. When standing, it is helpful to position yourself at an angle rather than directly in front of the other person. This is sometimes difficult to do, especially if he or she has 'collared' you and is demanding your attention by standing close up and directly in front of you, practically poking you in the chest! Even if you move sideways slightly, the other person will sometimes move with you so as to remain in front of you.

In the listening context, the aim is to show that you are giving the other person space so that she feels able to talk and share with you what she is worried about. This is a two-way process, and messages will be sent back and forth from both or all involved. Sometimes the messages are confused or are interpreted wrongly, by either party. But we have to keep on trying to create the right conditions for talking and listening to take place. The messages given and received through body language, also referred to as non-verbal communication (NVC), will determine, to some extent, the course of the session.

Note-taking
What do you, the listener, do about note-taking? The trouble is that there can be few things worse than trying to talk to someone who is constantly scribbling away on a notepad. He may be looking at you sometimes, but even if he looks at you most of the time you are aware of a hand trying to write things down. The other question that the listener needs to ask is:

'What is done with whatever is written down and does it go on any records or in any files? If so, where, and who will see it?'

Part of the problem is that some people are anxious and think that they will forget information:

'Will I be able to remember what they tell me?'

There is not necessarily anything wrong in taking notes. However, in general helping and listening in the workplace it is not recommended that notes be taken, unless they are necessary as part of a process that might include some kind of disciplinary action, or there is a need to take down a telephone number, name or address. If you do need to write something down, then tell the other person that you are going to do it, and why:

'I'm sorry to stop you there, but I need to take down the name and address you have just mentioned so that, with your permission, I can telephone or write to them later [writes down the information]. Sorry, you were saying that you were having problems with . . .'

'I hope you don't mind, but I have this form to fill in so perhaps we can do this first. It's just information for my personal files, and I keep them locked away in my private cabinet. Nobody else has access to them and, if you wish to, you can read what I have put down.'

Tape-recording
Occasionally, professional counsellors, psychiatrists, psychologists and psychotherapists use tape-recorders to record a session, but even then, only a few choose to do so. In any case, this will only be done with the permission of those involved. When asking for permission, the counsellor or therapist will give a reason for wanting to do so. Often the reason is that he or she wishes to listen to the tape later in order to further understand what is going on.

One problem is that a tape-recorder is usually visible, or there is a microphone, and these can detract from the informality and intimacy of the session and result in the client or speaker being very much aware of their presence.

But there is no doubt that a tape-recording of her client's story can be of use to the counsellor. By listening to it over and over again she may be able to understand the problems better. It may be more difficult to use a tape-recorder, even a very small one, in a shop or factory than in an office. Here a tape-recorder was used with a couple who were having problems:

> He was very quiet and hardly said a word, while she was very aggressive and never stopped talking. Even the listener couldn't get a word in edgeways. She talked for almost an hour, while her partner and the listener just sat there looking exasperated. At one stage, her partner said that he wished he had a tape-recorder so that she could hear what she sounded like and how it was for him. She replied that they could use one if he wanted to. It was suggested that the first half-hour of the next session should be recorded, and she agreed. When the tape was played back and she heard herself, she shouted for the recorder to be turned off. 'Do I really sound like that?' she said. Her partner smiled for the first time, replied 'Yes', and then began to tell her what he thought of her behaviour. She realised what she had been doing, and *he* knew that he switched off when she started talking and retreated into himself. When they began to talk together, they both realised that theirs was not a one-way communication system. *He* had contributed to the relationship by his silence and backing off, although he had hitherto thought of himself as the 'innocent party' and had attached the major blame to his loud and extrovert wife.

Here the tape-recorder was useful in acting as a catalyst for them both to see what they were doing in their relationship.

Although, clearly, they do sometimes have a use, as a general rule a tape-recorder is not recommended as a tool for listeners and helpers in the workplace.

It is worth pointing out here that the particular listening skills we will be looking at later actually help the listener to remember information. Also, you don't have to remember all the details, and with experience it becomes easier, anyway. But what you can do is to note what the essential elements are in the story. You are not a tape-recorder, but a person who hopes to be able to respond to what is being said and to the feelings expressed. If the floodgates open and masses of information pour out, don't try to remember everything—let it come, and then, at a suitable point, go back to the beginning of the story and use the skills of paraphrasing, reflecting and summarising (to be explained in Chapter 10). You may not remember everything, but you will be aware of the main elements and of the feelings that have emerged. If you do take notes, keep them locked away and be aware of the rights of the individual over confidential and recorded information.

Confidentiality

Many people will not ask you about confidentiality, and having asked to see you will launch straight into their story. It is helpful to make it known to them from the beginning exactly where you stand on this issue. Some listeners will say that they offer total confidentiality—but this needs to be looked at carefully. You *can* offer total confidentiality, and even when ordered by a court of law to disclose the information you can still refuse to do so. But this may be taken as contempt of court and can lead to a fine or imprisonment. So confidentiality is usually offered under the following rules, which state that as a result of the information obtained in the listening or counselling session:

- no harm is likely to come to the individual;
- no harm is likely to come to others;
- no harm is likely to come to society in general;
- no illegal act has been or is likely to be committed.

The difficulty is that the information given could have relevance to the role of the employee at work. For example, someone who works on aeroplanes as an engineer or fitter may be an alcoholic or be severely depressed. This could affect his work and put the lives of others at risk.

Companies should have a policy about confidentiality, and this policy should be made clear to everyone. They should say whether or not they will keep records and who will have access to them. There is also the issue of what is sometimes called 'peer reporting', where information is handed on by a colleague. If there is a report from one member of staff, for instance, of sexual harassment against another member, should this be taken seriously or considered to be just gossip? Should it be acted on, or ignored until reported by the individual concerned?

It is useful for managers and supervisors to have a good working knowledge of the following Acts:

Health and Safety Act (1974)
Employment of Disabled Persons Act (1958)
Sex Discrimination Act (1975)
Race Relations Act (1976)
Employment Protection Act (1978)
Employment Act (1989)

There are also rules about 'freedom of information', setting out clients' rights concerning access to files and other records.

In the normal course of listening in the workplace— whether between manager or supervisor and another member of staff, or between one colleague and another—there may be no need to outline the rules of confidentiality, and all that may be required is for the listener to listen and encourage the other person to find his or her own solution. However, if it becomes apparent that a regulation or the law has been broken, then the rules of confidentiality may need to be made clear to the person with the problem.

10   The Essential Listening Skills

Hearing is not the same as listening. To say, 'I am listening to you' implies that I am making some kind of effort. In the process, sounds are being sent to the brain, but we can filter out, consciously or unconsciously, what we don't want to hear. I can learn to blank out the voice of a nagging wife or a moaning husband. I can keep saying, 'Yes, dear', but not be listening. I hear, but I don't listen. If the children are constantly asking a mother for things, she can switch off and ignore them, no matter how much they persist. This ability to turn off our listening and filter out sounds and information is something we develop over the years.

If what is being said is important to us, interesting or sensational, we immediately begin to tune in:

> I remember sitting on a bus and hearing two women talking in the seats behind. I was not listening, but could hear their voices in the background. Suddenly I was switched on to the conversation when I heard one say to the other, 'Yes, I've told my husband. The more you use it, the bigger it gets.' Straight away I was listening, but never did discover what they were talking about . . .

A woman I know well can go with her husband to a restaurant and carry on a perfectly normal conversation with him throughout the evening. Then when they leave, she gives him all the details of conversations at the other tables around them:

> 'Did you see that couple at the table on your right? Well, she's his secretary and he was old enough to be her father. He was telling her that his wife doesn't understand him and

they are staying in the same hotel at a conference. Did you
see the other couple opposite? She's just been in hospital
for a hysterectomy and their only daughter is expecting
their first grandchild, and . . .'

Some people can listen to a wide variety of things at the
same time.

Sometimes it depends upon what you are used to hearing:

A farmer up from the country was visiting his brother in
London and they were walking down Oxford Street. Suddenly the farmer stopped and said, 'Listen, I can hear a
cricket chirping.' 'Never in the world,' said his brother, 'not
with all this noise going on.' The farmer looked around and
there on a window-box outside one of the department stores
was a cricket singing away. 'Fancy hearing that,' said the
brother, 'How remarkable.' 'That's not unusual,' said the
farmer, 'It depends what you are used to. Watch this.' He
took a fifty-pence piece from his pocket and dropped it on
the pavement. They were both nearly knocked over in the
rush . . .

Similarly, a mother can be fast asleep and ignore even loud
sounds from outside, but if her baby makes the slightest
noise she is immediately wide awake.

Real listening is therefore not a passive activity, but must
involve concentration and focusing. When we are asleep we
can suddenly be switched on by a fire alarm or other loud
noise, but if we are with someone who wishes to talk to us
at length we may have to make a real effort to listen. Of
course, it depends on who it is and what he or she has to
say. If it is my son and he is in some kind of trouble, I
probably won't have to make much effort to listen to him. If
it is my neighbour making his usual complaint about my
cat, then I can easily put my brain into neutral and nod
occasionally with a feigned look of interest and concern on
my face. Underneath, I am thinking, 'Why don't you just go
away?' I think it, but I don't say it.

Those in positions where they are expected to listen—

such as clergy, doctors, nurses, social workers, shop assistants, hairdressers, beauticians, managers, supervisors and officials—cannot easily get away with pretending to listen. Because they expect them to listen, their clients, customers and patients can often tell when they aren't listening.

Real listening as a helper or counsellor, called 'active listening', requires a great deal of effort and skill. It is an activity that demands both physical and mental involvement at a deep level. As far as possible, the listener has to focus his or her attention entirely on the speaker, to the exclusion of everything else. It also calls for the application of specific skills—skills that are not new to us but that we are learning throughout our lives:

1 *Prompting* Includes verbal and non-verbal communication (NVC), and uses encouragement and the observation of body language.
2 *Mirroring* Feeding back to the speaker exactly the same words and phrases used by him or her.
3 *Paraphrasing* Here the listener uses different words and phrases to say the same things as the speaker.
4 *Reflecting* The listener reflects the feelings being expressed, both hidden and overt.
5 *Summarising* The skill of summing up clearly and concisely what has been said.
6 *Asking questions* The listener asks 'open' rather than 'closed' questions.

Some have developed these skills better than others, but we can all expand them.

ACTIVE LISTENING

Having settled comfortably, and being ready to listen, you need to ask:

'What is the best way I can listen to this person?'

In active listening you, the listener, respond to whatever comes across from the speaker. This involves the nature of the place where you meet, including how comfortable, or otherwise, it is: this, plus the way you respond, will determine what messages the other person gets from you, what messages you get from her, and whether or not and in what way she is able to talk about the problem. The skills of listening help you to show the other person that you are really listening, and encourage both of you to move through the three-stage model of listening and responding: from *exploration*, through *understanding* to *action* (see pages 139–47). You cannot be passive in this, because everything you do and say will influence what happens. You are what some would call a 'catalyst', an 'enabler', because you can affect to some extent what the other person says and how she says it, and what she decides to do about her problems.

These skills have a definite purpose:

1   *They show that you, the listener, are listening and trying to understand*   The other person can see that you are listening because you are not sitting like a statue, but reacting physically and verbally. If you were not listening, there would be little or no response, and everything about you would be telling the speaker, 'I'm not listening to you.' The process should enable the speaker to say:

'You are using my words and expressions and then substituting your own equivalents, so you must be listening.'

Your response will show that you are making an effort to understand what she is saying and why she is saying it.

2   *They help the client to be clearer and more precise*   Your response to the individual helps him to sort out the confusion he brings, and focuses on specific problems and feelings. If he is talking about a certain aspect of a problem, and you mention this particular aspect and ask about it, then you are helping him to concentrate on this as an issue. You are not being vague or generalising:

'You said you were, to quote your own words, "having problems with my supervisor". Perhaps you could tell me what kinds of problems they are?'

This focuses the problems more clearly in the mind of the speaker.

3 *They check your understanding of the problems* They ensure that you, the listener, are getting the story right:

'You said that it was a problem concerning a colleague at work and also a problem affecting your home life?'
'That's right, it is to do with a colleague, and my partner tells me he's getting tired of hearing about her, but it also affects the children because I'm angry about her all the time when I'm at home.'

4 *They check the client's understanding* When a person has a problem, to hear himself speaking through someone else can be very revealing and mean that he begins to see himself and his problems in a different light:

'You said you hated him and can't stand him any longer?'
'I didn't say I hated him, did I? Well, I suppose I did, but that sounds a bit strong, especially when we've been together so long. Mind you, as I think about that, I suppose it's true. I do hate him.'

5 *They give direction to the session* They prevent the speaker from just rambling on aimlessly and jumping from subject to subject. The skills help her to focus on one problem at a time rather than on a lot all at once:

'You said you had problems with a colleague at work, but also that you recently had a hysterectomy and were divorced nine months ago. Perhaps you could tell me more about the divorce, as this seemed to come first?'
'Which of these three would you like to talk about—the divorce, the hysterectomy or the problems with your colleague?'

6 *They give time for reflection*   While the client is talking, you are listening and thinking, and while you are
responding verbally, she is given time to think. The skills
remove the pressure for either of you to think that you have
to talk all the time. While you are speaking, your client
might be thinking:

> 'Yes, that's right. But I'm not sure about this, and I don't
> know if it's true. I need to think about this some more.
> Shall I tell her about that other problem? I'll wait and see
> what she says first and whether or not I feel I can trust
> her.'

THE LISTENING SKILLS

1 Prompting

The first task of a listener is to encourage the other person
to speak. Some may not need much encouragement, but
others will be silent and not know where to begin. Therefore you must try to make them feel at ease. Show that you
are interested, but relaxed and not anxious or on edge; that
you are calm, confident and reasonably still, but not sitting
frozen to the chair. Prompting can be both verbal and
non-verbal: it is done verbally through the words we use,
and non-verbally by how we react physically. If you have a
form to complete first, this can break the ice, but you will
need to say what the form is, why you need it and to what
extent it is confidential.

It usually helps if you begin by making the other person
welcome and comfortable and by offering him tea or coffee,
if available. You may need to make a number of things clear
before you start:

Confidentiality   The client should know whether or not he
can talk to you without your telling anyone else (see pages
169–70). Tell him that, if you have to disclose things, you
will ask his permission, unless it is a matter where the law
has been broken. You may have to say that if certain things

are disclosed that affect you, others or the job in ways that are important to the organisation, then you may have no choice but to tell someone else. This needs to be conveyed in a sympathetic and sensitive manner, so a lot depends on how you say it.

Unhelpful approach:

'I have to tell you that I'm under certain obligations to the firm, so if you tell me anything questionable then I'm going straight to the manager, whether you like it or not. I have no choice.'

Helpful approach:

'You probably realise that I have to work under certain rules, and although I hope that you will feel able to tell me whatever you wish, you might tell me some things that affect other people. Normally the question of breaking confidentiality would arise only if you were to say that you were going to harm yourself or someone else, or if you were to tell me something that involved the law having been broken. But we can discuss this, if you wish, should it arise. Do you want to ask me anything about this before we begin?'

You could mention specific things like child abuse, but usually when you refer to confidentiality in a sensible manner the response is:

'Oh, no. It's nothing like that.'

In most instances, people with problems will come along expecting that what they tell you will be treated as confidential and that you will not make it general knowledge or the subject of gossip. They may not expect a long explanation about confidentiality, but by making things clear from the beginning future misunderstandings can be avoided. What people do want is to feel that they can trust you. Perhaps that's why they have come to you in the first place?

Time   It is essential that your client knows from the beginning how much time you have available (see pages 159–60). You may say that you have all the time in the world, or that you have an hour but that she can make another appointment if she wants to:

> 'You remember when you first spoke to me, I said we had an hour and then I've to go to a meeting at eleven, but we can make another appointment if you decide to do so. Is that all right with you?'

It is sometimes helpful if you say something about leaving time for a summing up of what has happened during the session:

> 'We have an hour to talk, but it may help if I let you know when we have ten minutes left so that we can look at what's happened and decide where we go from here, and whether or not we need another session. How do you feel about that?'

Less formal sessions may take place on the shop floor rather than in an office, and the time factor may never arise. But what will affect even an informal session is if you suddenly look at your watch, even if this is nothing more than a reflex action. The speaker may think:

> 'She's just looked at her watch. Perhaps she's bored and in a hurry, or maybe she's not really listening.'

The purpose   As a listener, you are not there to tell the other person what to do, and you should say so at the beginning. You hope that through what happens in the session he will be enabled to make his own decisions and see his own way through his problems:

> 'I ought to say something about how I see this session. As I see it, I am not here to tell you what to do, although it is usual for some people to feel that they want me to do that. My job is to help you to look at the problems as far

as you want to and to see where they have come from and what the causes might be. Also, we should be able to look at the future so that you can decide what you can do.'

Pain and difficulty You may need to explain that he may find it difficult to know what to say because he doesn't know you well, and that he may find it painful to talk about his problems:

'As we don't know each other very well, you may find it difficult to talk or to know what to say. Also, if you are talking about some painful areas of your life, you may find it very difficult.'

Alternatively, if you work with a person or are responsible for him you probably know him quite well already—which can be a mixed blessing. If he knows you he has probably come because he trusts you in some way and thinks that you will listen and can help. On the other hand, he may come to you and then, because you do know him, not want you to know too much about him. It is quite common for a person to come and tell you his or her problems, and then feel so embarrassed that he or she ignores you and avoids you ever after. If you do feel that this might be a problem, you can probably refer him to someone he doesn't know with whom he might feel more comfortable about talking.

The session begins

Start by saying that you are pleased she has come, and offer her a cup of tea or coffee, perhaps. You could also give a word of encouragement, and even a gentle smile. But not a grin or grimace—when you wish to talk seriously to someone there can be few things worse than that person grinning at you all the time. The opposite also applies, of course—do not wear a miserable expression. Look accepting and concerned, but not worried. 'Concern' and 'worry' are very different things, and to look 'worried' is clearly not a good idea in this context! The word 'concern' is from the Latin meaning 'to sift or discern', so a concerned look indicates that you are ready to discover why the individual has come and what the problems are.

At the beginning, you might say something about smoking. This is an activity that is becoming more and more unacceptable in our society, but since some people, including listeners, do smoke, the subject will need to be addressed. Also, those who do smoke will probably smoke more when they are under stress. The simplest thing to do is to ask if she smokes, or say that you do, and then come to some agreement about it. If you both smoke, this could offer an opening that helps to create a more relaxed atmosphere. In some organisations there are rules about where you can and cannot smoke.

You might ask her to come into your office or room, and then shake hands with her. Some polite remarks may be made about the weather or whatever may come to mind—*something*, at any rate, to make her feel at ease. However, you must not dominate her either with your presence or by talking too much. The atmosphere needs to be a calm and accepting one:

> 'It's good to see you, Mrs Jones, and I'm pleased you've come. I understand that you wanted to see me about some problems you are having at present. Perhaps you could tell me something about them.'
> 'Well, Margaret, it's nice to see you again. You said, when you telephoned, that you were having some problems. Where would you like to begin?'
> 'Good morning, Mr Young. My name is Joan Elwood and I'm the welfare officer [supervisor, manager or whatever]. Perhaps you could tell me why you have come and what the problems are?'

If she is silent and restrained, or looks nervous:

'It seems to be difficult for you to know where to begin, so perhaps you can tell me why you have come? There's no hurry, so just take it slowly and begin where you feel you are able.'

If she is clearly finding it difficult, then acknowledge it straightforwardly by saying so. If she looks as though she is about to burst into tears, again, acknowledge it:

'This seems to be hard for you. You look very upset.'

It is important to tune in to whatever the other person is feeling. A box of tissues on the table nearby tells her that it is all right to cry and prevents the embarrassment of not having a handkerchief if she does. It might also be important to sit quietly rather than press her to begin:

'You seem to be finding it hard to know what to say. If you are not sure where to begin, perhaps you could sit quietly until you feel able to tell me why you have come. We aren't in a hurry so take your time.'

The problem with too long a silence is that it can be very threatening to have someone opposite you who is saying nothing, particularly if he or she is just sitting looking at you. In practice, acknowledging a difficulty helps the client to feel that you understand something about how she feels, and it often leads on to talking. If her reaction is to burst into tears, offer her the tissues and, if you feel it appropriate, tell her gently that it is all right for her to cry. If you know her reasonably well, you can, if you are near enough, put your arm around her or just touch her arm or shoulder. As a general rule, do not get out of your chair and go to her and hug her unless you know her well enough to do so. When people are crying and embarrassed it can make things worse to have someone get up and come over to them. Some like to be left alone when they cry, and if you do go towards them may ask you to leave them alone. There can also be problems if one party is a man and the other a woman. It is better to acknowledge very quietly what is happening and tell them they can cry, and then wait until they have stopped.

It is important to think about how you actually speak. For example, you can put the accent on any one or more words. Try this sentence:

'Where would you like to begin?'

Then, as an exercise, say it aloud stressing a different word each time:

'*Where* do you want to begin?'
'Where *do* you want to begin?'
'Where do *you* want to begin?'
'Where do you *want* to begin?'
'Where do you want to *begin*?'

Each way you say it conveys a different meaning. Also, if you alter the inflection and tone of your voice, this too changes the meaning. The inflection of the sentence can rise slightly, remain quite flat or drop towards the end. The tone can vary from sounding gentle and accepting to harsh, critical or impatient. This applies, of course, to everything you say throughout the session, and needs to be constantly kept in mind. Take just one word, such as 'Hello': depending on my tone and inflection, this can sound hard and aggressive or calm and warm. If I raise the inflection at the end of the word or phrase, it moves into becoming a question.

Once the session has started and the client has begun to talk, you need to encourage him or her further. You need not say much more than the minimum:

'Um.' 'Uhuh.' 'Yes.' 'No.' 'Ah-ah.' 'Yeah.' 'Right.'

This kind of thing can be said with slight movements of the head, but not vigorous nodding or shaking. Also, you can make even these utterances in different ways, your tone and inflection conveying totally different meanings. You can say, 'Oh,' in a fairly level way that does not sound threatening, but if you raise your voice it becomes a question, and can even indicate surprise or shock. How much surprise or shock is shown depends on how it is said:

shocked	'Uuuuuuum'	—	voice rising high
surprised	'Uuuum'	—	voice rising slightly
uninterested	'Um'	—	voice flat or dropping

In the early stages of a session it is better to use a particularly quiet approach and a gentle voice.

These short words prompt at a minimal level, and enable the client to know that you are interested; you are responding in a way that means that you are listening. However, you must not use the single-word response in an inappropriate way:

'I've come to see you because my wife has just left me.'
'Good.' 'Right.' 'Yes.' 'I see.'

The response might well be:

'What do you mean, "good"? What's good about it?'
' "Right"? I don't think it's right, do you?'
'You said, "yes". Do you know something I don't know? Has somebody been gossiping?'
'You said, "I see". What do you see, exactly, and what do you know?'

The point is to use this minimum-level response in such a way as to encourage him or her to open up. It is a simple skill, but one we can neglect because of our urgent desire to do something and move ahead as quickly as possible. It is all too easy to feel that:

'Sitting and listening is not enough. I must find a solution.'

Everything you say and do will influence the course of the session, and by prompting you are doing something positive and active. As already mentioned, it is usual at the beginning of a session to allow the other person time to gather his thoughts. Prompting can help you to determine whether or not he feels able to trust you and let you into his world. Put out of your mind the desire to find solutions and, instead, focus your attention on the other person here and now. As he speaks, prompt him gently with your simple words, 'Yes', 'Uhuh', 'Um'—but beware of using them too often, or inappropriately:

> When I started listening-skills training we televised role-plays and watched ourselves acting as both clients and listeners. I was appalled because every few seconds I was saying, 'Yes, Yes', over and over again. Not only was I saying 'Yes', but it was coming out very quickly and sharply and clipped short. Also, I had a tendency to nod my head every time I spoke. Although I was an experienced helper and carer, I did wonder how many people I had put off over the years.

So we need to be aware, not only of the words we utter, but also of how we say them and of our own behaviour when we are speaking. Ask yourself:

> 'Do I have any habits that might detract from the listening process? Do I nod frequently, sniff, move a hand, arm or leg over and over again, twitch, blink, wink or do anything else that is unhelpful?'

Perhaps you could bear this in mind next time you are listening to someone.

> Anne was a good listener, but when she was listening she would not only nod her head, but give a kind of bow towards the person and make a movement of her mouth which was more a grimace than a smile. She thought this was helping the other person to see that she was interested. In fact, others tended to think, 'Why is she doing that? She's just like a mother hen.'

> Derek was a clergyman who was really caring and kindly, but he had the bad habit of endlessly repeating the same

word—'actually'—which cropped up (at least once) in every sentence. He would say, 'Where actually would you actually like to begin?'; and then, when prompting, 'I see, actually', 'Yes, actually' and so on. It was very off-putting for parishioners.

Perhaps the only consolation when we do get it wrong, or make unhelpful responses either verbally or non-verbally, is that people are sometimes in such a state that they are unaware, to begin with, of how we are responding. But what kind of consolation or excuse is that! The other point is that, if we do get it wrong, even if they don't actually tell us, we will know it from the way they speak and behave—if we are listening actively!

2 Mirroring

Like prompting, this is a relatively simple skill, but it requires great sensitivity to get it right. Mirroring is the skill of 'playing back' the *same* words or phrases used by the speaker. It can be a simple one-word response, or a phrase or part of a sentence that he or she uses; and you, the listener, feed it back almost like a tape-recorder would.

One-word responses   The speaker may use a sentence in which one or more words are significant:

'I'm feeling very angry with my colleague.'

Possible response:

'Angry.'

Or slightly longer, but, again, using the same word or words that the speaker uses:

'You say you're feeling angry.'
'You say you're feeling angry with a colleague.'

This can be said in a flat, gentle tone of voice:

'Angry.'
'You say you're angry.'

Make sure that if you use a flat tone it does not sound threatening or as though you are not interested.

Alternatively, you can raise the inflection slightly at the end of the word or sentence so that it is asked in a questioning manner:

'Angry?'

Or you can drop the inflection if you feel that it is a very highly charged word, and so make it less liable to sound threatening. Other significant single words might be 'alone', 'mother', 'husband', 'children', 'money', or anything else that the client says that sounds important to him—perhaps a person, a group of people, a thing or a feeling:

'I need to talk to someone because I'm having problems.'
'Problems? What kinds of problems are you having?'
'Well, I'm having problems with someone at work.'

Possible response:

'Problems with someone.' *or* 'Problems with someone?'
'Problems at work.' *or* 'Problems at work?'
'Problems with someone at work.' *or* 'Problems with someone at work?'

The question mark makes all the difference to the meaning conveyed.

The response may be more complicated when 'feeling' words are included:

'My boss makes me livid when he laughs at me.'

Here there are a number of single words that are important: 'boss', 'livid', 'laughs' and 'me'. Any one of these can be mirrored, but you need to pick the one that seems more important from the way the individual says it. If it is said tearfully, then you could concentrate on 'laughs' and say:

'Laughs at you.'
'You say he laughs at you.'

If it is said in an angry manner you could pick out the word, 'livid':

'Livid.'
'Livid?'
'You say he makes you livid.'
'You say he makes you livid?'

Again, note the use of the question mark and the difference it makes. If you mirrored the word 'boss', this would tend to concentrate his response on this particular person and he might then go on to tell you more about what his boss does that is so troublesome to him.

Words and phrases An extension of the one-word response, the task here is to pick out longer words and phrases and feed them back:

'The children are getting me down all the time and I just can't cope.'
'The children are getting you down and you feel you are unable to cope?'

The response could be split:

'Getting you down? All of the time? And you say you can't cope?'

The problem with mirroring when we look at it in isolation from a real situation is that it can sound irritating. If I have told you that I am having problems with money and you say, 'Money?' or 'You say you're having problems with money?', I might reply:

'I said money, didn't I? Aren't you listening? You sound just like a parrot.'

Strangely enough, in practice it rarely works out like this, and often people will go on to tell you something more about what they have said:

> 'I'm having problems with money and don't seem to be able to manage.'
> 'You say you're having money problems and don't seem to be able to manage?'
> 'That's right. You see, we bought a new house recently and the mortgage has just gone up and my husband has lost his job and . . .'

The mirroring skill is useful in the early stages of a session, when the person doesn't know what to say or how much she can tell you or trust you, and so gives you a gentle hint to test your response:

> 'I want to talk to you about my supervisor. He's always on my back and I just get so angry and upset when he has a go at me. He just seems to pick on me, and I get the impression that he wants to get rid of me. If he did that I don't know how I would manage at home. We rely on my salary to get us through each month and couldn't cope without it. Also, the other people at work wonder what's going on, and one of them has told me that it is because underneath it all he fancies me . . .'

But mirroring can be misused. Imagine what might happen if you mirrored this, saying:

> 'Your supervisor.'

The speaker would probably be very angry, wonder what on earth you were saying the word for and look at you as though you were stupid. The point is that this example would require a longer response than mirroring just a word or phrase.

Be aware of mirroring as a response, and use it when appropriate. In practice you will find you use it not only at the beginning, but also at intervals throughout the session as and when necessary. Mirroring is a kind of prompting, except that the words you use are theirs and not yours. It is also useful to listen for 'feeling' words, but you need to know when it is safe to use them. It can be very threatening to mirror 'feeling' words at the beginning of a session, when the individual doesn't know you very well and may be anxious or wary.

3 Paraphrasing

Unlike mirroring, where you use the same word or phrase as the speaker, paraphrasing means using different words to say the same things. It is an extension of mirroring, in that you take in the words being used, but then you use your own words to say what you think the other person is saying. Paraphrasing, in the listening-skills context, concentrates on the content of the story rather than on the meaning:

What story is this person telling you? What is it about?

The aim is to keep away from feelings, even though this is sometimes difficult, and occasionally impossible, to do. Paraphrasing responses may be short or long. Take this example:

'You see, it gets me down when he harasses me constantly at work. He won't leave me alone and is at me all the time. It makes me feel very angry and vulnerable.'

Short:

'So he's getting at you all the time, and this makes it very difficult for you.'

Long:

'You are saying that this man at work constantly seems to be tormenting you and is always there on your back, and that this just gets at you and makes it very difficult for you.'

A response to a longer story would be to shorten it, picking out the main points and substituting as many of your client's words as possible with your own. Remember to try to avoid the feelings at this stage:

'I get into work every morning and my supervisor is there all the time, even following me around whenever he can. I've never done anything to harm him and for some reason or other he just has to make my life a nightmare every day. He constantly gets at me in the smallest ways, and even though I and my colleagues have told him to leave me alone he just won't. It's as though I've done something wrong and he just has to go on about the slightest things. He criticises my hair and my clothes as well as telling me how useless I am in my work. I just can't stand it and want to do something about it. That's why I've come to you.'

You could paraphrase it like this:

'You are saying that you have a problem with your supervisor, who seems to be making your life a misery. He complains about your work all the time and also makes personal comments as well as being on your back whenever he can. You've had enough of this and want to take some kind of action.'

And you could add:

'Have I got the story right so far?'

At this stage you are not looking for solutions or asking searching questions, but simply telling her story in a different way. What this says to her is that you are listening; you couldn't be telling her story if you weren't. Also, you are taking the time and trouble not only to listen to her story, but you are filtering it through your mind and putting it into your own words. The other person is also listening to the story through you, and this helps her to know you are trying to understand. Also, she is being given the chance to check out what she has told you, thus gaining a better understanding of her predicament. If the response works, she may move on to tell you more:

'That's right. That's just how it is. But he is also a neighbour. He lives a couple of houses from us and I think he is jealous of me and my family. I'm not *sure* why, but I think I know.'

If it doesn't work and she remains silent, you can paraphrase again in a different way just to check the story again, and see what response you get. She might reply by saying simply:

'Yes, that's right.'

You could then ask a question—and the possibilities for asking questions are extensive. We will look at asking questions later, but here are some possible responses:

'Tell me more about your supervisor.'
'You said he gets at you all the time. Perhaps you can tell me more about that and give me an example?'
'What kind of a relationship have you had with him in the past?'
'When did he start being like this with you?'
'In what ways does he get at you?'
'Tell me more about the ways in which he gets at you.'
'What does he do and say when you ask him about this and tell him to stop?'
'You said that your colleagues have spoken to him about it. What have they said to him and what was his response?'

Remember that early in the session it is better to concentrate on some of her first statements rather than asking how she feels or what she thinks she can do about it. This should come later—unless she bursts into tears, which you would need to acknowledge there and then. Even so, it would probably be inappropriate to concentrate on this emotional response.

The secret of paraphrasing lies partly in finding words from your own experience and vocabulary that you think say the same things the other person is saying. Try to come up with words that do not sound alarming, threatening, frightening or critical. Your response at this stage must not put undue pressure on this person. This is why you are still steering clear of feelings because, if she became threatened in any way or began to feel more insecure, she might either switch off and tell you only superficial things, or get up and leave.

Consider this case:

'My husband has recently started to drink a lot, and when he's had a few he comes in and . . . I'm worried about him. The children don't know what's happening, and I have to be careful what I say and do and leave him alone until he comes round.'

A wrong way to paraphrase:

'I see. So your husband is an alcoholic and you and the children are terrified of him?'

To this the client's response might well be:

'I didn't say he was an alcoholic, unless you know something I don't know. And we aren't terrified of him, either. He's a good father. It's just that he's been out of work for a while, and he worries about it and feels awful that he can't support us.'

Or even:

'How dare you say that about our family? We've always done our best for the children. He's a good husband and father, so don't you say that he's an alcoholic. You don't even know him, anyway.'

Here you have made two assumptions: that he's an alcoholic and that the rest of the family are frightened of him. She didn't say that. You might even find that what you say, inaccurate as it is, is accepted, especially if you have a responsible position:

> 'Do you think he's an alcoholic? I've not thought of it like that before. You're the expert, so you may be right. Will he need treatment, do you think, and what should I do? Do you think we will have to leave him?'

The saving grace of getting it wrong is that the client will almost always tell you, or give you a hint by what she says or how she behaves:

> 'Well, I didn't say he was an alcoholic, did I? I'm sure he hasn't got to that stage yet, but it still makes it difficult for us all.'

You now have another chance to get it right, so go back to what she said and check it out again:

> 'I'm sorry about that, but it's just that you seemed so upset. You said that he recently started drinking. Tell me when this first started.'

A better paraphrasing response would be:

> 'You say that your husband drinks more than he should. This influences how he behaves and it affects both you and the children.'

Here you have not asked any questions, but made a statement and repeated in your own words what she has said. You must make sure that your interpretation of the story is as accurate as possible, and without making judgements.

As in prompting and mirroring, you need to be careful about the tone and inflection of your voice. Remember that by changing the inflection in a word or sentence you can change the meaning completely. You would probably avoid eliciting an indignant response if you said in a fairly flat manner that the husband was an alcoholic and that they were all frightened of him, and if your tone suggested that this might be her interpretation too:

'You seem worried that he might be becoming an alcoholic?'

Even if you are wrong, the likelihood is that she will think about it and reply along the lines of:

'No, I don't think he is. That's not my main worry. I am concerned because he's been out of work for so long.'

Also, how you interpret it depends to some extent on how she tells you the story. She may look worried, sit on the edge of her seat and blurt it out in tears, anger or exasperation. He *might* be an alcoholic, or that may be her worry, but the point is that at this early stage of the session you need to check out further what she is saying rather than say what you think she might be implying. This is why it is better at this point to stick to the story and look at the content rather than the meaning or the feelings. Even if she has come to hate him and has decided to leave, she may not wish to acknowledge this just yet.

Just as with mirroring, you need to concentrate hard on what your client is saying. Remember that your paraphrase should be shorter than her original words—otherwise, you will have done most of the talking.

When she is listening to your paraphrase she will be hearing her story, probably for the first time, from someone else. She may be thinking:

'Is that what I said, that he drinks a lot? Does he? I don't know, but he doesn't get drunk. Is this my main worry? Is it to do with the children? How do they fit into this? What is my main concern?'

Even in the early stages of the session, you are getting her to talk and think and are helping her to see what the important elements are. You are helping her to sort out the confusion of facts and feelings.

4   Reflecting

Reflecting moves to a deeper level because it begins to look at the feelings, whether expressed or hidden away. Hopefully, the client has started to settle down a little and you have shown by your prompting, mirroring and paraphrasing that you are listening and are willing to hear what she is saying. She should begin to feel that she can trust you as she gradually opens up her life and feelings to you—not very deeply, perhaps, but she is beginning to look below the surface and let you see what lies underneath. She may also begin to see or feel things she has never seen or felt before and did not know were there.

We need now to look at this important question:

Which are more important, facts or feelings?

There is sometimes a division between what we know in our heads and what we feel in our hearts. Of course the separation of functions is not anatomically correct, but we sometimes use this kind of language to describe what is happening to us and how we feel. We speak of our hearts being more concerned with feelings than with facts. For some ancient peoples the gut was the seat of the emotions, and we still say, 'I can feel it in my stomach' or 'I have this gut feeling.' When emotions well up inside us, concerning ourselves or other people or situations, we sometimes find it unsatisfactory to use conventional language to describe them. In order to express what we feel, we may use the symbolic language of swearing, perhaps including Anglo-Saxon expletives, or we may use picture language and images:

'My husband is a b****y animal.'
'The children are monsters.'
'My mother-in-law is an old battle-axe.'
'I hate my boss. He's a b*****d.'
'My wife is nothing but a selfish cow.'
'He makes me feel as though I'm just a piece of dirt.'
'He treats me like a dog.'

These statements are not literally true, but they do convey a wealth of feeling. This feeling can be increased by the way we make the statements. We can express our feelings not only with words, but with our whole bodies. Any of the above statements can be made calmly and quietly; but they can also be spat out in anger and frustration, delivered with popping eyes, clenched jaws and fists, and ears practically steaming.

The content of the story, that you were dealing with when you paraphrased, may hide the feelings that lie beneath the surface, but these will usually emerge in some way. Take the following account, delivered in a calm voice:

> 'My husband came home the other day and said that he had bought a new car. He hadn't asked me what I thought about it, but just said that he'd done it. He knows I wanted a hatchback, but he's bought a large saloon. I suppose I don't mind, but I thought it was a bit unfair of him and said so, especially as I also go out to work and it's part of my money he's using. Still, he's the man, isn't he? But I do drive the car as much as he does, if not more, and he could have asked me first. He does things like that often, without asking for my opinion. It's the same with our annual holiday. We always go where he wants.'

Though the content here is easy to describe, the feelings are partly hidden—but not completely, and this person's story does give some clues as to what she may really feel:

> 'I suppose I don't mind.'
> 'He's the man [long pause], isn't he?'
> 'It's part of my money he's using.'
> 'I do drive the car as much as he does, if not more.'
> 'He could have asked me first.'
> 'He does things like that often.'

The image coming across is of someone who is probably very angry about her husband's behaviour, who feels belittled, and who resents strongly the fact that he ignores what she would like. The same statement could have been made with knuckles clenched and a look of dejection or anger on her face. It could have started off quietly, but her inflection and tone could have changed gradually until her voice finally reached a crescendo of anger and frustration.

You, the listener, need to listen to what is said, but also to how it is said.

What are the main 'feeling words' in this sentence?

'I baked him a cake just before he died.'

What does the act of baking a cake represent? Is it love and caring, and trying to do something in a hopeless situation in which you feel utterly helpless because someone you care for is dying? It can be an attempt to substitute order and hope for confusion and despair. Almost every word can be a feeling word:

'I'	'It was something I did myself. It was personal from me to him.'
'baked'	'It was something I did when I was helpless.'
'him'	'It was for him because I loved him.'
'a cake'	'This was his favourite cake and I know he appreciated it.'
'before'	'We knew he was dying. The doctor had just told us.'
'he died'	'His life was snuffed out like a candle and it was so unfair and unjust and I'll never see him again.'

What has the person said, how has she said it, and what has she not said? Why did she go on for so long and never mention her husband or the children or that she has lost her job or that she has just come out of hospital? Facial expressions and body language will also convey a meaning.

'My wife is rather selfish, I know, and never seems to bother with how I feel, but I don't mind it a bit really. I do love her, in spite of it, although I know that some would feel upset and angry if they were in my shoes.'

What is he really saying?

The skill of reflecting feelings depends on your use of synonyms to replace the speaker's words—for example:

love   liking, enjoyment, friendship, fondness, fancy, desire, passion, infatuation, worship

tired   slow, dull, sleepy, drowsy, lethargic, heavy, sick of, fatigued, exhausted

angry   upset, resentful, discontented, annoyed, cross, ratty, exasperated, irate, mad, furious

A good exercise is to sit down, think of a feeling word and then write down as many words as possible with a similar meaning. Then, write them down again in ascending order of the amount of feeling they express. Put the words on a line running from the left (least amount of feeling) to the right (greater amount of feeling). With the word 'happy' you could put:

content, pleased, merry, delighted, thrilled, joyful, jubilant, ecstatic.

When your client is speaking, listen carefully, note the main feelings being expressed in his words and the way they are said, and in the accompanying body language. Then feed back the feeling or feelings. Your client tells you:

'I went to the doctor to tell him that I felt ill and he just sat there, gave me some tablets and told me to go home.'

Possible paraphrase:

'When you told the doctor that you were not very well he sent you home with some pills.'

Possible ways of reflecting:

'You saw the doctor because you were feeling unwell, but

you were upset when he just sent you home with some tablets.'

'It sounds as though you were very angry about the way the doctor treated you.'

'You seem to be very sad and depressed about the way the doctor treated you. It was as though he didn't have time for you and hadn't even listened to what was wrong.'

These reflecting responses could also be put as questions, by injecting a slight rise into your voice towards the end.

Feelings can be reflected at different intensities, depending on the amount of feeling that the individual with the problem expresses. Reflecting must not be done too heavily, yet must not trivialise his story or seem to be saying that it doesn't much matter. If I say I am very, very depressed, it is useless telling me that I don't look or act depressed, or to say that I look a bit 'upset' or appear to be 'under the weather'. If I am truly depressed, this could make me feel that you don't understand or believe what I say. If I say that I am 'a bit cheesed off' with my work and you say that I look terrible or that I must want to 'pack it all in', then I will feel here too that you haven't listened and certainly have not understood me.

Remember that when you are listening to someone you have to frequently ask yourself, 'How does this person feel?', then look inside yourself and try to find words that are as close as possible to the feelings that he is expressing. Your client says:

'I was upset when he said that to me.'

You can focus on the words:

'It seems that you were cross about what he said to you?'
'So you were annoyed with him when he said that?'

Or you can focus on the body language:

'You seem to be very distressed by that.'

'You were clenching your teeth when you said that, and you look extremely angry.'

Or you can focus on both the words *and* the body language:

'You said you were upset, but you look very angry.'

Reflecting also means that you move from sympathy to empathy (see page 129). You begin to reflect from within you what the other person is saying and expressing. You are attempting to take the step of moving from your world into his. To use earlier images, your two icebergs have collided and are grinding together beneath the surface; or you are moving from under your umbrella to stand with him in the rain.

When you reflect feelings, you are also moving forward in the task of showing that you are listening. Hopefully, when you are listening, the person with the problems will be able to say:

'You must be listening because not only have you nodded and made encouraging noises, you have used my own words. But you have also told me my story in your own words and you got it right, so you must be listening. It felt a bit strange to hear my story through you, but it has helped me to be clearer in my own mind. You have taken the time and trouble to turn my problems around in your mind and shown me that you are trying to understand. Also, you seem to understand because you appear to know something of how I feel and you haven't criticised me or stopped me from getting angry or from expressing how I feel. You have helped me to understand myself better and have given me the opportunity to think.'

If you have done these things, you are really listening, and by reflecting the other person's feelings you are helping him to discover a way through the turmoil of his problems.

5 Summarising

Using the skills of active listening, you have prompted your
client to talk to you; mirrored her exact words; used your
own words in paraphrasing; and reflected the feelings that
she has expressed. You have let her know that you are
responding, not just by showing that you are interested in
her and being friendly but also by being able to reflect
something of her inner world from within yourself. However, in spite of your positive response to her you still need
to ask:

'Have I really understood what she has said?'

The earlier skills have helped you to check that you have
been getting the story right and are beginning to understand,
but how far *do* you understand? To check this you use the
skill of summarising—the technique of playing back to the
client the story, as you have heard it, as accurately, clearly
and concisely as possible. Summarising permits you to
check out not only what you think you have been told, but
whether you have picked up any feelings, either expressed
or hidden. The word 'think' is important here because the
listening process is about interpretation. We hear a story,
ask about it and then translate it not only in terms of what
we have heard but also in terms of our own thoughts,
experiences and feelings. You can begin by saying:

'Let me just check this out, if I may . . .'
'Let me see if I've got the story right so far. What you
have been telling me is . . .'
'Perhaps I can go over what you have said . . .'
'It would help if I could just check what you have told
me . . .'
'OK. You've said that . . .'

If the individual has been talking for about twenty minutes
or more, you should sum up everything that has been said.
If she has been talking for a shorter time, a kind of
mini-summarising, similar to paraphrasing, could be used.

You can paraphrase regularly to sum up short stretches, but summarising will give a broader picture and it usually includes more than one element of the story. The only problem is that if you summarise too frequently it can be irritating for the client.

Using the various skills outlined so far, you have been listening to a story from Sarah, and now you need to summarise. Note that the summary is split into five separate stories, or packages:

'Let me just check this to see if I understand what you have been telling me. You have told me a great deal and I would like to see if I have got the story right.

You have been married for sixteen years to Ted and have three children, a boy of sixteen, a girl of thirteen and another boy of ten. Your husband works in a local factory and you work here as a clerical assistant. You have told me that you think part of the problem is that you and your husband hardly ever see each other and that he spends most of his free time going out with his friends. You have grown distant from each other and the relationship is very strained.

Also, you say that you are having problems with one of your children. Michael seems to be very unhappy at school. You're not sure, but you think he is finding it difficult to decide whether or not to stay on at school for another two years and go to university. He tells you that he doesn't get on with his tutor, but you wonder if that's just an excuse because his best friend is leaving school at the end of this term and already has a job lined up.

Another problem is that you are worried about your job here, especially as some of your colleagues have been made redundant and you wonder if you will be next. This would cause financial problems for you as you rely on your money to make ends meet.

You have also said that your mother, who is a widow, is ill and lives in the north of England, and even though you have a sister who lives near her you are not sure that she will look after her, as they don't get on. Your mother has been asking if you can go and take care of her, but that's an impossibility and it makes you feel awful that you are unable to help. You feel responsible for her, but angry about your sister's lack of interest.

You also tell me that you have met a man here at work, and although you tell him you are only friends he seems to think it's more than that. You've been speaking to him just for someone to talk to, but he wants to take it further. There seems to be some confusion about your feelings for him, but you say that it's not serious from your point of view—at least, you don't think so.

Is that right so far?'

Sarah:

'Yes, that's right, and I'm all mixed up in my mind. I just don't know how I can sort it all out.'

You:

'Perhaps you could tell me which of these you think is the most important to you now?'

Sarah:

'Well, I'm not worried so much about Michael. He'll cope and make up his own mind if we don't push him too far. My mother will just have to get on with it as I think she's not seriously ill, probably just missing dad—he died last year. My main worry is my marriage. This other man, Brian, told me that he thinks my husband knows about us. I don't know how, but Brian thinks someone here at work has seen us talking and has told Ted. Also, Brian is married and has children so I don't want him to get the wrong idea. I do like him. He's good company and has listened to my problems and been very supportive, but I have mixed feelings about it. If we were both free, that would be a different thing, but we both have marriages and children. Brian has told me that he has seen Ted in a pub with another woman, but I'm not sure if he's telling me the truth. Also, there are some women here at work who have told me that Brian isn't all he seems to be, and that he's tried it on with others. I don't know what to think.'

When you have summarised, hopefully two things will happen. First, your client will tell you whether your version is accurate; and, second, she will go on and tell you more. In the above case, Sarah's first response might simply have been:

'Yes. That's right.'

You could then have gone on and prompted, paraphrased, or reflected feelings:

'You say you're not really worried about Michael and your mother at present. They'll manage. Perhaps you could tell me more about you and Brian—how you met, and what the relationship is like between you now?'

or:

'Your main concern seems to be your marriage to Ted. Tell me more about how things are between you.'

or:

'It seems that you have doubts about Brian, even though he's been very supportive. You're not sure if he is being honest with you.'

or:

'You're concerned because your relationship with Ted isn't working out at present, and you feel that your marriage is important. You want to sort it out, but are not sure how Ted feels about you. Brian was there when you needed someone and did listen, but you feel that he has more than this in mind. There is also some confusion and doubt about what he has told you, and you're unsure about what other women at work tell you about him.'

These responses are not questions. They are statements about what Sarah has said and requests for her to talk further. You can turn them into questions by slightly raising the inflection of your voice towards the end.

Since one of the aims of summarising is to confirm that you are listening and that you understand what you are being told, you should not be vague. In Sarah's case, it would have been unhelpful to offer a summary like this:

'I think I've got the story right. You said you are having problems with your husband. You're not sure, but you think that he might be having an affair. Also, you've met a man who fancies you and you don't know what to do and whether or not to leave your husband. Then there's something about your children. Did you say you had two or was it three? One of them wants to leave school and get a job, but you would prefer him to stay on and go to university. Your mother is seriously ill and you don't get on with her very well, but feel guilty about it. But your main worry is that you think you might love this other man. Is that about right?'

Certainly not! You've got it very wrong and will have given the impression that you weren't listening; that you don't really care and are not really interested. Sarah may be very angry about your response and express it, or she may just retreat into a shell:

(angrily) 'I didn't say that at all. I never said I loved him—and his name is Brian. My main worry is about Ted and our relationship. Weren't you listening to me?'

or:

(resigned and distant) 'I suppose so.'

The 'suppose so' should give you the clue that she does not

'suppose so' at all, and that you need to start again. If you do get the summary wrong, the person you are trying to help may simply sit there and acknowledge what you say, but then switch off, believing that you are not really listening. Or she may get up and walk out in despair or disgust.

It is worth stressing that summarising requires the ability to pick up feelings and to set out the problems in a clear and systematic way. Often when people come for help they are confused, so a precise summary can help them to put their muddled thoughts and feelings into some kind of order.

Sometimes when you have summarised, a client will deny what she has told you and become very angry and upset. This does not necessarily mean that you have summarised inaccurately, but that the client has not liked what she hears herself saying through you. But it can lead to a genuine acknowledgement of the underlying feelings and to real dialogue:

> A young married couple came to see me because they were having difficulties in their relationship and thinking about separating. They didn't want to do this because they both felt that they did love each other very much. The wife said that she had had, and was having, a number of relationships with other men in addition to her husband, and had done so since shortly after their marriage two years ago. Nothing sexual had happened, but she just felt the need to go out with other men. She said she didn't really want to stop because she enjoyed it; she felt that her husband didn't mind, and she didn't care either. I then asked him how he felt about this, and he said in a very quiet voice, 'I just want her to be happy.' She was very calm and cool in telling the story, and as she did so she kept looking at him. He sat there and said nothing, even when she directed questions at him. She showed no anger or emotion whatsoever as she talked.
>
> I then summarised in a very clear and matter-of-fact way, saying that she had said that she didn't care. She became very angry and upset, claiming that what I had said was not true. She then said that she did care, and turned on him and shouted and swore at him.

At this, he suddenly changed and sat bolt upright in his chair. Her denial of my summary and her change from being calm and cool to getting angry had shocked him into reacting. Although he found it painful, he began to say that he did care about her and hated it when she went out without him. He too became angry and upset and, perhaps for the first time in their relationship, she began to feel that he did care and did love her. His lack of reaction had been taken as a lack of caring or concern. They began to talk to each other, and gradually their underlying feelings began to emerge. All the pent-up anger in them both burst out and they were able to begin to say what they really felt.

Summarising helps both you and the other person to check out her story, and if you do it accurately she may begin to see things in a new light. It should enable both you and her to look at what has been said and expressed, and it creates the possibility of looking at what has not been said or expressed. It prevents her from jumping from one problem to another and mixing up all the associated feelings. You outline the areas of concern, and then focus on which ones she is able to talk about further:

'So, there are a number of problems here: your husband and your desire to make the marriage work, this other man and what he wants and tells you, your son Michael and his schooling, and your mother's illness. Which of them do you feel you can talk about?'

As with the other skills, summarising gives the other person time to think about her problems and then to decide what she can tell you.

There are two main occasions when you can usefully summarise :

1 when the other person has talked for a long time and then becomes stuck, or stops;
2 when you are stuck and don't know where to go next.

A very helpful general rule is:

'When in doubt and you don't know what to do, summarise.'

For instance, you have been listening to a long story and the individual suddenly stops, perhaps because he has finished or because he simply doesn't know what to say next. As the listener, you may think (and feel):

'Where do I go from here, and what do I say next? I am confused and don't know what to do.'

Go back to what you have heard. Recall the story you have been told and tell it back to him as clearly as you can. Try to sort it out into headings and packages, with each part containing one of the elements in the story. You might include the feelings, either those expressed or those that you think are hidden below the surface. You may also need to say something about the state the other person is in:

'You stopped there, and perhaps you are finding it difficult to talk and tell me what the problems are. It seems as though you are embarrassed and don't know if you can trust me.'

Instead of reassuring him that he can trust you and go ahead and tell you his problems, you might say:

'Well, let me see if I have got your story right. What you have told me so far is . . .'

Then go on and summarise.

It is rather like 'putting your cards on the table' or, as already suggested, sorting things into packages. Each card or package represents a particular problem, and you try to associate the facts and feelings with the relevant package. It isn't *quite* as simple as this, because often the problems are interlinked. As far as possible, summarising should attempt to sort them out as distinct problems, while linking them where necessary.

6 Asking questions

This is a skill used throughout the session, and it is important to get it right. In the initial stages you may not be asking
many direct questions, but, as we have seen, even a prompting word such as 'husband' can be put in a questioning way
by changing the inflection and tone of your voice:

'Husband?'

When people are talking they don't always say what they
mean: sometimes they tell you what they think you want to
hear, or what they feel they can tell you at that time. They
may tell you the story entirely from their own point of view,
with a few embellishments—usually in their favour. It is the
truth, but through their eyes only. What is true, especially in
relationships or when people have problems, is often a
matter of perception rather than what we would normally
call 'fact':

He says: 'She's an old cow.'
She says: 'He's a pig.'

They are both right, from their own perspective. Asking
questions is one way of trying to establish what the truth is
for the person or persons concerned. It can help them to
face up to the implications of what they are saying.

If you ask the wrong questions, you can frighten the
individual away, threaten him or make him retreat into
himself. The following could be said critically, aggressively, unsympathetically or in any other inappropriate
manner:

'So, when did you start having all these affairs?'
'Why on earth did you take all that money and spend it
like that?'
'Do you always behave irresponsibly and get drunk?'
'So you thought you could get away with it and your wife
wouldn't find out, did you?'
'When she said that to you and you were angry, you

were obviously being stupid. Didn't you think about the consequences?'
'Don't you think that was a stupid thing to do?'
'You can't cope with your boss. Why not?'
'Why don't you like your work? What's wrong with it?'

Bear in mind that these questions can also be posed in a sensitive and caring way, but may still elicit very strong reactions.

There are basically two kinds of question: closed questions, and open questions.

1   Closed questions
Questions that usually require either information or a specific answer—sometimes as simple as 'Yes' or 'No'. Some examples:

'How many children do you have?'
'Where do you live and what is your address and telephone number?'
'When did you move to London?'
'How long have you worked here?'
'What job were you doing immediately before you came to work here?'
'How many pints of beer do you drink in a night?'
'How often do you go to the cinema?'
'Do you like your supervisor?'
'Do you get on with your colleagues at work?'

Closed questions are therefore questions that seem to close the options for replying, that do not allow the client to expand on the issue. They are useful when, for instance, you are filling in a form, but they can stop dialogue dead:

'How long have you been married to Ted?'
'Sixteen years.'

The reply *could* be longer:

'Sixteen years, and it seems like a hundred, the way he behaves, especially now that he just ignores me. And, because Michael is sixteen, you have probably guessed that we had to get married.'

But the probability is that the reply will be short and precise, and you then have to move on and ask another question:

'How long have you been married?'
'Sixteen years.'
'Have they been happy years?'
'No.'
'Never happy?'
'No.'
'So they've been mostly miserable, have they?'
'Yes.'

These are all closed questions, each receiving a closed answer. By their very nature, they limit the amount of information that can be given. If I ask how long you have been married, there is only one reply, unless you have been married a number of times before. Furthermore, a series of closed questions can sound like an interrogation, and make the client close up and decide to tell you only 'closed' things.

Closed questions usually begin with:

How much . . .?	How many . . .?
Where do you . . .?	Did you . . .?
Are you . . .?	Does your . . .?
Do you . . .?	Will you . . .?
When do you . . .?	How often do you . . .?

These *could* bring a lengthy reply, but unless you just want specific pieces of information it is better to phrase such questions in a different manner.

In practice you will find that when a relationship of trust has been built up, you will probably receive a longer reply to closed questions. If your client is opening up and feeling able to talk to you, and goes on to give you more than the basic closed reply, you might ask:

'Why do you think that was?'

This raises the issue of 'Why?' questions. In general, these are unhelpful because the individual often does not know why. That may be precisely why she has come to you.

'I don't love my husband any more.'
'Why?'
'I don't know. If I knew the answer to that I wouldn't be here.'

If you ask someone to make a simple statement and to then answer everything you ask, and you proceed to ask 'Why?' every time he replies, a number of things can happen:

'I think the weather has been awful lately.'
'Why?'
'Because it has rained a lot.'
'Why?'
'Because there have been dark clouds coming from the west.'
'Why?'
'Because there have been anticyclones coming in from the Atlantic.'
'Why?'
'Because the weather men have said so.'
'Why?'
'Because they are on the telly.'
'Why?'
'I don't know, do I? Probably because they are paid to do so.'
'Why?'
'I don't know . . .'

When you repeat the question 'Why?', the speaker is thrown further and further back into looking for explanations and reasons, and eventually he runs out of answers. He may just dry up, or he may become angry. He may lose track of what he was saying, and even forget what the original problem or question was. He may burst out laughing with embarrassment, or start shouting with rage:

'Why are you asking me all these stupid questions?'

He is being pushed into a corner and put under pressure to find a reply, and may eventually become defensive and hostile. He may even just stop talking and remain silent. 'Why?' questions give you little information or help, and they give no scope for your client to think further than the simple answer.

Other common replies to closed questions, apart from 'Yes' and 'No', are 'I don't know', 'Don't ask me', 'How should I know?', 'I can't answer that', 'I'm not going to tell you', or even 'Mind your own business.'

One of the problems with a closed question is that it can mean that you do most of the talking and that you then have to ask another question. Also, it's not very imaginative and can give the client the impression that you don't know how to listen and help. Worst of all, it can seem like an interrogation.

2   Open questions

Questions that allow the other person to give a wide-ranging response and to focus on particular problems or feelings. To use the iceberg analogy from Chapter 7—whereas closed questions normally derive their answers from the top of the iceberg, open questions encourage the client to search for reactions, thoughts, emotions and experiences that lie not only just below the surface but also at a deeper level.

Examples of closed questions:

'Do you get on with your sister?'
'Yes.'
'Do you like your sister?'
'No.'

Turning these into open questions:

'How do you get on with your sister?'
'Tell me how you get on with your sister.'
'How do you feel about your sister?'
'In what ways do you get on with your sister?'
'Tell me about your relationship with your sister.'

You *could* still receive a closed reply to any of these, such as:

'I get on all right with her.'
'Not very well.'
'Not much.'
'I don't know.'
'I'm not going to tell you.'

But you are more likely to receive an open reply to an open question.

Take this series of closed questions:

'How long have you been married?'
'Ten years.'
'How many children do you have?'
'Four.'
'Boys or girls?'
'Two boys and two girls.'
'What does your husband do?'
'He's a plumber.'
'Where does he work?'
'He's self-employed.'
'Where do you live?'
'On the other side of town.'
'How long have you lived there?'
'Five years.'

This has been a two-way conversation with each person talking, but the listener has talked almost twice as much as the client. You can get most, if not all, of this information by asking one question:

'Tell me something about your family, your children and husband, how long you have been married, where you live and how long you have lived here.'

It is a complicated 'open' question, but it contains what you want to ask and leaves the response to the client. You can then sit back and listen and let her talk, and she will have talked much more than you have. This helps her to be, and to feel that she is, the focus of the session:

'Oh—well, we have been married ten years and have known each other since we were at school together. We have four children. Mandy is eight, Carole six, Richard four and the baby, Carl, is just two years old. We live on the other side of town in Brampton and moved here five years ago from Birmingham. My husband, Ken, is a plumber and works self-employed, although he's finding it difficult to get enough work.'

More examples of open and closed questions:

Closed: 'Do you love your husband?'
Open: 'How do you feel about your relationship with your husband?'
          'Tell me about your relationship with your husband.'
          'What are your feelings for your husband?'
          'Tell me how you get on with your husband?'

More specific open questions:

          'Tell me what happens when your husband comes in after work.'
          'Tell me what happens when you and your husband have disagreements.'
Closed: 'How many children do you have?'
Open: 'Perhaps you could tell me something about your children?'
          'Tell me about the children.'
Closed: 'Did you go to work yesterday?'

Open: 'It would help if you could tell me what you
           did yesterday.'
           'What did you do yesterday?'
Closed: 'Do you argue a lot with your wife?'
Open: 'In what ways do you and your wife not get on?'
           'When you argue with your wife, what
           happens?'
Closed: 'Do you like your work?'
Open: 'What feelings do you have about your work?'
           'How do you feel about your work?'
           'Tell me about your work and how you get on
           in the factory.'

Open questions begin with:

'In what way [ways] do you [are you] . . .?'
'How do you feel about . . .?'
'Tell me what happens when . . .'
'Tell me about . . .'
'What do you mean when you say . . .?'
'What feelings do you have when . . .?'
'When that happened, what did you do [think/say/
feel] . . .?'

Strictly speaking, 'Tell me . . .' is not a question, but it has a
questioning meaning. It asks the person concerned to think
about his reply, invites more information and encourages
him to tell you more of the story.

Mirroring, paraphrasing, reflecting and summarising can
all take the form of questions:

Mirroring: 'Angry?'   'Happy?'   'Disgusted?'
                'Broken?' 'Your husband?' 'Work?'
                'Pointless?'
Paraphrasing: 'You said you were walking down the
                street when you saw this woman you
                know well, but she ignored you and
                walked straight past you. What did you
                think [feel] about that?'

Reflecting: 'This seemed to make you very angry, and you then lost your temper with your supervisor?' (inflection rising)

Summarising: 'You have told me a great deal about your wife and what you see as her constant nagging and how you just don't seem to be able to get on with her. You also mentioned having problems with your boss at work and your feeling that he doesn't like you for some reason unknown to you, and you are afraid of being made redundant. You also said that you have been spending more than you earn and your wife doesn't know it yet. These seem to be the main areas. First, perhaps you could tell me more about your relationship with your wife?'

Having summarised in this way, you could end by asking a number of questions:

'Tell me which of these is the most important to you and the greatest worry.'

'You said that your boss doesn't like you. What does he do to give you this impression?'

'You mention financial worries. How much do you owe [closed question] and how do you think your wife will react when she finds out [open question]?'

Even a single word can be an open question—again, depending on how you use the inflection and tone of your voice. However you ask the question, it should be phrased in a non-judgemental, non-critical and non-threatening way. To make a judgement means that you set yourself above the other person; to be critical suggests that you know better than she does; to be threatening is possibly to frighten her away or silence her:

'Don't you think you were stupid to have said that?'

'Weren't you wrong to have acted in that way?'

'That was a silly thing to do, wasn't it?'

'Angry?' (in a very surprised way, suggesting to her that she shouldn't have been angry)

'You shouted at him?' (in a shocked manner)

'Ran away?' (with disgust)

'Leave him?' (in a flat voice suggesting that you don't agree with what she is thinking of doing)

The aim of asking questions is not just to get information, but also to help people to explore their world and uncover what has happened and how they feel about it, so that they understand more about their situation. You, the listener, need to be sensitive to their state of mind and mood and be aware of which questions are likely to be most appropriate at the time. It does not mean that you should not ask probing questions, or even disturbing ones. It means that the questions should be relevant to what is being said. It is a good idea to ask:

'Why am I asking this question?'

Unless you are simply wanting information, try to pose all questions as open ones. This gives your client an opportunity to explore his response and to look inside himself, thus enabling both you and him to know more of his world.

Encouraging people to talk, mirroring, paraphrasing, reflecting feelings, summarising and asking open questions are basic to all good listening and are used throughout the three-stage approach (see pages 138–47), particularly in Stage 1. Most listeners may not need to move beyond Stage 1—often, by this point, the client will have been given enough help to be able to sort things out in his mind. Your skilled listening will have helped him to gain a clearer notion of what his problems are and may have given him some idea of what to do about them. At the very least, he will know that someone cares, is approachable, and is available whenever he needs a listener.

11 Further Skills

In addition to prompting, paraphrasing, reflecting feelings, summarising and asking questions, Stages 2 and 3 of the three-stage approach, Understanding and Action, use special skills that help to give the client a better grasp of his situation and problems and enable him to make decisions about what to do about them. The in-depth study and use of these extra skills is normally reserved for the trained counsellor, but there is no great mystery about them and they can be used, if to a limited extent, by any good listener.

STAGE 2 SKILLS: UNDERSTANDING

These skills, like those of Stage 1, have particular aims:

- to show that you, the listener, are understanding more;
- to challenge the speaker;
- to help the speaker to see patterns and inconsistencies;
- to help both him and you to see the situation more clearly;
- to help to develop self-understanding;
- to help to show what is happening between listener and speaker;
- to look at possible goals and decisions.

The skills concern showing deeper empathy; challenging and looking at recurring themes and inconsistencies; giving information; looking at the interaction between listener and speaker; setting goals and making decisions.

1   Showing deeper empathy

Here you, the listener, begin to move towards a much deeper understanding of the client and her situation and problems, and the client often realises this. In the examination of Stage 1 skills, empathy was used rather than just sympathy, and here empathy is used again, but at a much deeper level.

In counselling the counsellor needs to have a clear understanding of him- or herself, and part of counselling training looks at personal hidden agendas. In other words, what does the counsellor need to know about himself in order to help the client? What are the counsellor's prejudices, beliefs, attitudes, experiences, preferences and moral values, and how might these influence what happens in a counselling session? As Chapter 7 showed, this holds true not only for counsellors, but for anyone who attempts to help through listening.

If I have a deep fear and dislike of dogs, or my neighbour's dog has for years barked for long periods every morning and evening and today he tells me that the dog is sick or has died, I am not likely to be very sympathetic. My own experiences and feelings interfere with my ability to show sympathy. Or it might be a question of a previous experience such as divorce:

> Jane was a supervisor in an office. She was thirty years old, had one child, Matthew aged four, and had been divorced for two years. It had been a particularly difficult and distressing time for her, and many scars and a great deal of anger, guilt and resentment remained from the experience. However, she managed well on her own and Matthew attended a pre-school group every day. She had not remarried and felt very bitter about men in general.
>
> One day, Sandra, who worked with her, came and asked if she could have a word in private. Jane took Sandra to her office. Sandra began to talk about her problems and eventually revealed that she was having great difficulty in her marriage and didn't know what to do. She talked about her

husband's behaviour and how they were drifting apart. They had a small child, and she believed she should stay with her husband and wanted to sort out her problems. She had read in a newspaper recently that it was better for parents to stay together for the sake of the children, than to separate. She felt that they still loved each other, but were going through a bad patch. What was she to do?

Jane began to feel the pain from her own divorce surging up inside, and tried to push the feelings down. She was a good listener and used the Stage 1 listening skills, but found it increasingly difficult to know what to say or do. Her own feelings began to take over, and when Sandra asked her what she should do Jane said that it was probably time for Sandra to make major changes in her life. 'Marriage is all a matter of chance,' she said. 'If it doesn't work out, then you should make choices and move on in your life. Separation or divorce is not the end.' This was her own experience; she had coped, she told Sandra, and so could Sandra if she only had the courage to make up her mind about what she wanted.

It is common, after a difficult experience, for people to have the attitude:

'I coped and am coping, and so should you. I've been through it myself and know what it's all about.'

Jane made a number of mistakes. She found it impossible not to let her own experiences take over and influence what she said. She was unable to control or understand her own feelings and resorted to giving advice. She told Sandra what to do, and this advice was based on the experience of her own difficult divorce and on the fact that she had managed. She could see Sandra, just like herself, living on her own, with her little boy being looked after while she continued working. Her bitterness against men affected her attitude towards Sandra's husband and situation, and there was an element in her of not wanting Sandra to sort out her marriage:

'Why should she be happily married when I'm not? I failed and coped, and so can she. You can't trust men anyway, and even if she does seek marriage guidance help and stay with him, he'll probably let her down just like my husband let *me* down.'

Note that she refers to her 'husband' and not to her 'ex-husband'. She is still tied into the relationship and has been unable to let go. She is still going through the grief of her own marriage break-up, and in some ways is still locked very firmly into the feelings that were generated before, during and after her divorce. Jane could have listened carefully, kept her own feelings under control, and asked Sandra how she felt about going to Relate or to some other organisation or person for counselling. But Sandra's problems resurrected her own feelings, and she was unable to empathise in any way. This meant that she was unable to see, understand or feel that Sandra still loved her husband and wanted her marriage to work. The feelings that Jane projected on to her were totally inappropriate for Sandra's situation.

Those who are going through pain of their own and having problems in coming to terms with it, although they often think that they are ideally suited to help others, are in fact not likely to be much help at all—especially if the problems are similar. If I am going through a bereavement, major loss or life change this is likely to affect my attitude towards others with problems, whether similar or not. I need to have worked through my own difficulties to a successful stage of healing or acceptance before I can really listen to others and be of help. Marital counsellors will stop counselling if they are experiencing their own marital problems, separation or divorce. Cruse counsellors, too, will stop counselling for a time—two years or more, depending on the incident and how they are coping—if they experience a bereavement. Those who have *moved success-fully through* a similar difficulty, on the other hand, will often be able to express deep empathy. Remember, though, that even if you *have* had a similar experience, your feelings will be your own and no one else's will be exactly the same.

In deeper empathy the listener listens to the story and to what lies behind it and picks up signals about what the deeper feelings of the other person may be:

> 'You said that you were thinking of packing in your work because of the trouble between you and your boss, and you seem quite calm. But I wonder if you are also feeling resentful and angry about it?'

Here the listener is probing to discover what the deeper feelings might be. And her response is expressed as a question so that the client can choose to disagree or to acquiesce—and then, perhaps, to go on to describe these other feelings. Such a response shows the client that the listener is not just accepting things at face value, but is prepared to move to that deeper level where there may be pain and anger, or a host of other feelings. It also gives the client permission to express his feelings and to move through any doubts or uncertainties towards the point where he can trust the listener. He may even be fearing that she may not be able to cope with these feelings or that she will reject them by ignoring, criticising or trivialising them. The fact that she is showing this deeper empathy enables the client to see and feel that she is quite prepared to share something of his pain and accept it just as it is.

2 Challenging and looking at recurring themes and inconsistencies

Here you, the listener, look carefully for anything in the story that does not seem to fit in with what has emerged or with what is happening in the present. For instance, it might be that your client expresses a number of needs, ideas, feelings and wants that seem incompatible with each other. Take this extract from the long story of a woman who had very strict parents:

'I hated my parents for the way they treated me, and I don't want my daughter to hate me. I want to be nice to her, but she is surly and rude. She's only thirteen and I don't want her to think that she can stay out late at night. She is often out until well after midnight, and I get angry when she does this and ignores what I say.'

Here there are a number of statements:

'I had a hard upbringing and my parents were over-strict with me and I hated it—and them.'
'I don't want my daughter to hate me.'
'I want to show my daughter that I love her.'
'I want to stop her from staying out late at night.'
'If I am strict with her she might think I don't love her.'
'Her behaviour makes me angry.'

There is confusion and some contradiction in the story. Possible response from the listener:

'You say that you don't want your daughter to stay out late, and you don't want to be too soft with her. But you don't want her to think that you don't love her or care about her. Perhaps you are worried about losing control of her, or that she might get into trouble? You do love her, but know that she wants to stay out later than you think is sensible. You say also that she is very unhelpful at home. You did say that you came from a very strict background, and I wonder if there is some hint in all this of resenting the freedom she has?'

The listener needs to be careful, because it may be that the mother is right and needs to put her foot down more firmly or confront her daughter with her difficult behaviour. It may not be necessary to look at the mother's childhood—the daughter may just be going through a difficult stage. There are other possibilities: she might be pregnant, on drugs, in debt, in love, having her first sexual experiences, not wanting to be out of line with her friends who all stay out late, or she may be having problems at school. Perhaps she is just a difficult teenager who is taking advantage of her mother's fear of upsetting her? But if the listener has been really listening and believes that she detects some resentment in the mother that is affecting her attitude towards her daughter, then it needs to be raised as an issue.

Sometimes a person tells one story while her body language (see pages 161–6) is saying something else. For instance, she tells you how much she loves her work, but every time she mentions it she grits her teeth or clenches her jaw, or her knuckles go white or she avoids eye contact. You might say:

> 'You have told me a number of times that you love your work, but I notice that every time you speak about it you look down at the carpet and your hands grip the edge of the seat. Perhaps you can tell me what this is about?'

She might then tell you that she does indeed love her work, and then go on to say how awful it can be and how hard it is to cope. There could be a number of reasons for this: a difficult supervisor or manager; a colleague who is not supportive; sexual harassment or bullying at work; marital or financial problems at home; difficulties with the children; the menopause; a recent bereavement or major loss; a psychological or psychiatric problem; a drink problem; drugs; a neighbour. Any of these, or something else, or a combination of difficulties, might be the underlying problem. You, the listener, must try to elicit what the cause is, and be ready to challenge your client if she persists with the inconsistency:

> 'On the one hand you say that you love your work, but on the other you say that you find it awful at times and that you can't cope. How do you tie these two things together? What things are happening that make it difficult for you?'

It may be that she keeps mentioning a particular person,

thing or incident, or that there is a certain feeling around all the time. Your response might include a degree of empathy:

> 'You have been telling me about your problems here at work and you have also said that you are finding it difficult at home, but that you do manage to cope. You then talk about your mother who is ill and about your children. I seem to get the distinct impression when you are talking about all these things that there is something else troubling you. You talk quite calmly, but there is a catch in your voice and an underlying feeling of sadness coming across. Also, you are dressed rather sombrely and I wonder if there is some element of loss here for you?'

People need to be challenged so that they can sort out what the problems are and then put them into some kind of order and perspective. The listener is not just someone who listens and agrees and who never says anything that is challenging or difficult. However, when you do challenge a person by mentioning recurring themes or inconsistencies, be prepared for him possibly to become upset or angry. And bear in mind that these responses are part of his story and that you will never help him if they are not acknowledged. Also, if he thinks that you have not noticed the inconsistencies, he may think that he can just go on talking without moving to a deeper and possibly disturbing level. He may even see you as an 'easy touch', thinking that he can safely come and talk to you without tackling the real issues. To miss or ignore recurring themes and inconsistencies does not help the client to move forward, and you and he might become stuck in a particular way of relating. There is a notice somewhere in the Australian outback on a road full of holes and deep ruts:

> 'Be careful which rut you get into—you will be in it for the next two hundred miles.'

This is no less true of listening. In order to move forward you need to know what is happening to you as well as to

your client, and this may necessitate addressing issues that
are painful for both parties.

3 *Giving information*

This is a skill based on the listener's knowledge, and
includes the offering of information about possible sources
of help. For example, it could mean letting a client know
what the rules are about sickness or about confidentiality
within the organisation for which he works. Information
and advice can be given about such things as:

The organisation:	rules and regulations about such aspects as sickness, holidays and leave, welfare, confidentiality and policies
Divorce:	the legal situation, including a person's rights under the law; likely costs; housing; children
Benefits:	Social Security benefits for the unemployed and sick; allowances, pensions, etc.
Marital problems:	Relate and other counselling agencies
Bereavement:	Cruse, Compassionate Friends and like organisations
Training:	internal and external training opportunities

Ensure that the information you give is relevant, and be
careful not to do everything for the other person. Whenever
people can discover things for themselves, they should
be encouraged to do so. If the listener takes over all
responsibility from her client, his self-esteem and self-
confidence are liable to be diminished. He needs to feel that
he has some element of control over his own life. Being
encouraged to do something simple for himself, such as
going to the Citizens' Advice Bureau to find out who and
what is available to help locally, can help to restore some of
the confidence that he may have lost.

4   Looking at the interaction between listener and speaker
This skill is sometimes known as 'immediacy'. You, the listener, will already be looking at body language as well as listening to what is being said and how it is being said. It is also important to look at what is happening between you and the speaker. It may become apparent that something is going on beneath the surface that is not being directly addressed or brought out into the open. The other person is aware that there is a difficulty, and though he may not say it in so many words—and may not even know what it is—he is expressing it through the way he speaks and behaves. At the same time, he is picking up and interpreting messages from you. The point is that he may be angry or upset not only about his own problems, but with you, the listener. Look for the clues in the following case:

> Graham had been coming to see his supervisor, John, about some personal problems, and each time he came he always sat in the same chair. As there were only two chairs around the small coffee table, this meant that John also sat in the same chair. One day when John opened the door, Graham walked into the office, walked over to the chairs, sat very firmly in the supervisor's chair and folded his arms. At first John didn't know what to do, but felt slightly angry about it and said quietly to Graham, 'You're sitting in my chair.' 'Yes, I am,' said Graham. John sat in Graham's chair and realised that he felt very helpless and didn't know what to do or say. He asked Graham why he had done this. 'I wanted to see how it looked from your chair,' Graham replied.
>
> John became aware that Graham was very angry and upset and that it was something to do with him. Gradually, as they talked, John began to feel that Graham felt that he didn't understand. He said, 'I have the feeling that you think that it is all right for me to sit here and listen and that I don't have the first clue what it is like for you. And I think you are very angry with me for being your supervisor and, you think, not having any problems. Perhaps you wanted to sit in my chair because you see it as the seat of power?'

Graham's protest could have been about something else. He might have been making a statement about the fact that John had not told him what to do about his problem, but whatever it was, the fact of Graham sitting in John's chair was saying something very firmly about his perception of John and of what was happening between them. It was John's task to discover what this meant and to feed it back to him. Graham could have been sitting with his arms folded and a grin on his face, or looking sad, dejected, questioning, angry, upset or aggressive. In the event, he just sat there with an angry look that said:

'Get out of that one if you can, and see how it feels for you when you are sitting in my place.'

Possible responses in comparable situations:

'I get the impression from you that you are very upset with me and want to walk out of the room. Perhaps you feel that I don't really understand what you are saying or that I am not listening?'
'I am beginning to feel very annoyed with the way you are avoiding answering my questions. Whenever I ask you about your colleagues at work you change the subject. It feels as though you don't trust me and may even think that I am going to tell others about what you say. Or perhaps it is too difficult for you to talk about your colleagues?'
'I have the feeling that, for some reason, we are not getting on. There seems to be a block between us and I'm not sure what it is. It feels as though we are both fencing with each other. What do you think?'

The aim is for you, the listener, to ask yourself:

'What is happening between us?'

You can do this by asking two other questions, one focusing on the speaker, the other on you—and both on what is happening in the relationship:

1   'How do I think or feel the other person feels, and what is going on for and in him now?'
2   'How do I feel about this person and about what he is telling me, and what is happening in me now?'

The accent is on the word 'now':

'What is going on between us—now?'

Without understanding this 'immediacy', you will be unable to help your client to move forward. If it is not acknowledged and tackled, what is going on *now* can act as a block to exploration, understanding and looking at the future. Immediacy needs to be used in the listening process as a positive tool for creating a deeper relationship and understanding between listener and speaker.

Part of immediacy is sharing feelings, with you, the listener, saying what you are thinking and feeling at the time. Sometimes when you feel helpless, you are probably feeling what the speaker feels a lot of the time. In the situation just described, John had to sit in Graham's chair, and when he did he felt helpless. This may have reflected Graham's feeling that he was in a situation without hope. The same may apply to other feelings. When you are listening to a couple, you might reflect on what either or both are feeling about themselves or about each other. This is one way in which you can be honest and open with the speaker or speakers. To ignore thoughts and feelings coming across from one party to the other is to miss an important part of what is going on. Not least of all, it may prevent you, the listener, from helping.

5   Setting goals and making decisions
It may not always be possible for a listener to help an individual to consider goals. All she may be able to do is to help him to look at the problems and gain a better understanding of what they are, where they might have come from and how they are affecting him now. In many cases

referral will be the best course of action. But there will also be times when the listener can encourage the other person to look at what he may be able to do for himself, and what choices he may have.

It is difficult, if not impossible, to look effectively at goals unless there has been some clear understanding of the nature of the problems. According to the three-stage approach, understanding should follow on from using Stage 1 skills, whose aim is exploration. The listening skills from Stage 1 carry on into Stage 2 (understanding) and Stage 3 (action), and the skills of Stage 2 move into Stage 3. Remember, though, that these three stages are not distinct and have no clear boundaries. This is because human problems are not like separate beads on a string, either—they are almost always complicated, confused and interrelated. You may think in a specific case that you have outlined the problems clearly and summarised them precisely, but, as you move on, find that other problems and factors emerge which throw a different or new light on the scene. Also, it is difficult to look at goals unless these goals are stated clearly and precisely.

Take, for example, a reasonable and understandable goal such as:

'I would like to be happier.'

The trouble is that it is too general. It is the sort of statement that would be better made early in a session, so that there would be time to explore it—some understanding of the statement would need to be achieved before it could be seen as a possible goal. This example raises a number of questions:

'What do you mean by the word "happier"?'
'In what ways do you want to be happier?'
'What is it about your present life that makes you unhappy?'
'What things about your life now do you not like?'
'What things would you change in your life now, if you could, to make things happier?'

Statements more realistic than 'I would like to be happier':

'I would like to be happier in my marriage, because although we are both still in love we are drifting apart and there is no sex.'

'I would like to be happier at work because I find it rather boring and repetitive, and would like to do something where I can see the results of what I do.'

'I would like to be happier and get on better with others at work, but I tend to be a bit of a loner and when they ask me to join in with them or go out with them I am too shy, so don't go.'

'I would like to be happier and find someone to go out with and, possibly, fall in love. To have someone I cared for and who cared for me would make all the difference to my life. But I am afraid of making a relationship in case it breaks down and I then feel rejected.'

'I would like to be happier at work and have a better relationship with my boss. He tends to bully me, and I retreat into anger and silence.'

All these are statements that could lead to you, the listener, asking more questions and encouraging further exploration, which, in turn, should lead to better understanding.

Any possible goals must be realistic; appropriate; measurable and achievable.

(a) *Realistic goals*   There is no point in having goals that are not possible for me:

'I would like to look like Clint Eastwood.'

This is unrealistic if I am five feet six inches tall and ugly!
Here is a statement of facts, as I perceive them:

'I am unhappy at work, hate my present job, and don't get on with my colleagues. My marriage is in difficulties, my wife is unhappy and I have financial problems.'

I might have a number of desirable goals:

1 Change jobs and find work that I enjoy and that I could be happy in.
2 Be promoted and so have more money and more responsibility. This would help to alleviate my financial problems as well as taking me away from my present colleagues.
3 Ask for a transfer, and then have new colleagues and be able to start afresh. This might also involve moving house, and a new life for me and my wife—which might improve our relationship, as she doesn't like this area.
4 Go to Relate for marital help.
5 Win the football pools or lottery and become a millionaire, thereby solving all my problems.
6 Run away and start a new life for myself.

Of these six goals or choices:

(1) would be difficult because of the high unemployment in this area.
(2) is not possible because my reports have not been good and I haven't the right qualifications.
(3) might be possible, but I don't think it would help because the only transfer would be to Birmingham and my wife wouldn't want to live there.
(4) is not possible because my wife has refused to go to Relate with me.
(5) is wishful thinking.
(6) I just couldn't do.

I could choose (1) and look for a new job, but we have a mortgage and we couldn't afford it. I am not going to be promoted, so (2) is unrealistic. I don't want to go to Birmingham, so (3) is not what I want—it is possible, but not if my marriage is to survive. It would be stupid to choose (6) and run away, so although it would be possible it is not sensible, and doesn't fit in with my character. My only choice may be to go to Relate on my own (4) and hope that my wife will eventually come with me.

A more specific goal in this instance would be:

'I would like to find ways of getting on with my colleagues better, and feel that if I could be friendlier this would make all the difference. I would then be happier at work and, perhaps, happier at home.'

See how this next example of an inadequate and vague goal statement can be developed:

Vague goal:	'I want to be a better listener.'
	'In what way do you want to be a better listener?'
General goal:	'I want people who come to me to feel that I understand them.'
	'How can you achieve this?'
More specific:	'I could do it by learning to reflect feelings better, for I feel that this is one of my weaknesses as a listener.'
Specific goal:	'I want to learn to be able to reflect feelings better.'

Having started off vague, this now states a specific and realistic goal that I can probably achieve if I develop my skills in this area as a listener:

'I would like to be a better listener—I feel that I am not good at some of the skills. If I could reflect feelings more accurately, then people who come to me would know that I understand them better and we could move ahead.'

(b) *Appropriate goals* It is pointless having goals that are not within my range of values or beliefs, and that are neither possible, realistic nor appropriate for me.

Margaret, who is six feet tall and seventeen stones in weight, has said:

'I would like to be thinner.'

Again, this is too general a statement. As a goal it must be more specific, and it must be appropriate. It would be specific for her to say:

'I would like to weigh six stones.'

However, because she is very tall, this would not be appropriate. To weigh six stones would mean that she was either anorexic or extremely ill from some other cause. A more appropriate and specific goal for her would be:

'I would like to lose five stones in weight.'

At six feet in height, twelve stones would seem to be more appropriate.

Similarly, it would probably be inappropriate for some Roman Catholics to say:

'I would like to get divorced.'

This might be specific and achievable, but not acceptable within the belief framework of a given person. He or she might like to get divorced, but be unable to make the decision to do so. Consider this goal:

'I would like to be rich.'

This is probably not only unrealistic, but inappropriate, because the person making the statement has been unemployed for three years and has no qualifications or expertise. Furthermore, there are no jobs available where he lives. It is not a total impossibility, but inadequate as a possible goal for that person. More appropriate goals might be:

'I would like to learn to manage my money better.'
'I would like to learn a skill and get a job.'

Other examples of inappropriate goals:

'I would like to be Prime Minister.'

Earning the MBE might be a more adequate goal for me, so I could do extensive charity work in the hope that I will be recognised and rewarded.

'I want to be managing director of this firm.'

This might be possible in the future, but if I do not have the necessary qualities or credentials, then becoming a chief clerk or supervisor might be more appropriate for me.

> 'I want to produce twice as much work.'

This is inappropriate if I am already working almost as hard as I can. A more adequate goal might be:

> 'I want to produce ten per cent more.'

If I can do this by reorganising my work, it is realistic and appropriate.

(c) *Measurable and achievable goals* A goal must be capable of measurement so that I can say whether or not I have achieved it, and it helps if it is achievable within a certain time frame.

Margaret, six feet tall and seventeen stones, could say:

> 'I want to lose six stones in the next six months, and I am going to do this by having a chart and losing at least a stone each month.'

This is probably possible, realistic and appropriate. It is also measurable—it can be checked each week and month.

Consider this goal:

> 'I want to get to the top in my job.'

This might be unrealistic, not specific enough, inadequate and not achievable, but it is certainly measurable. I can tell how far up the hierarchy I am progressing because I am moving slowly up the scale of promotion. I may be satisfied with my stated goal, even though it is taking some time to achieve it.

And this one:

> 'I want to be happier at work. I want to change my attitude by being more friendly with my colleagues and joining in with them more.'

This is measurable because I can check whether or not I am happier at work. If I am more friendly and am not happier, then the goal was probably unrealistic, not adequate or not achievable. My colleagues may have decided to exclude me from their company for various reasons, or perhaps changing my attitude was not enough.

Stating a goal can make the individual think about whether or not it is possible, and how she can achieve it. Any particular goal may be realistic and possible for some, but not necessarily for her.

These Stage 2 skills can be used by any listener. They should help to create a better understanding of the problem and begin the process of moving towards making decisions and taking action.

STAGE 3 SKILLS: ACTION

The skills of Stage 3 move the client further towards making decisions. They embrace choices and goals, methods of achieving them, and the possible consequences for the client and for those around him or her. The skills concern problem-solving and decision-making, changing behaviour, evaluating the costs and consequences and endings.

These skills help the client look to the future. As with Stage 2 skills, the listener and speaker may not be able to make the key decisions and may have to be content with referral. But there are some fairly simple techniques that you, the listener, can learn with a view to helping your client to understand the situation better and to be more accepting, even if she can do nothing about it. These techniques might also help her to make decisions if the opportunity should arise—for instance, if her situation changed. Remember that, like Stage 1 skills, which continue to be used throughout the other two stages, the Stage 2 skills are also used into Stage 3. You should still be aware of the need to be empathic, to challenge the speaker by pinpointing the recurring themes and inconsistencies, to continue to give information, to look at what is happening between you and her, and to try to set goals. Stage 3 is concerned with achieving these goals and taking action:

> 'In Stages 1 and 2, you helped me to explore my situation and problems and I have begun to understand them better. Now you are trying to help me to make choices and take some kind of action.'

1   Problem-solving and decision-making

Once problems have been identified, there are a number of approaches to solving them.

(a)   Brainstorming

'Brainstorming' entails looking at as many solutions as possible, even those that seem ridiculous or stupid. The client writes down his ideas, and then examines them to see which are possible. Lateral thinking—extending one's thoughts and imagination as widely as possible—is useful here. Take this goal as an example:

> 'My boss is always getting at me and criticising me. I want to be able to deal with this.'

There are various possible 'solutions'. The person with this problem might:

- walk into his boss's office, and tell her exactly what he thinks of her; ask her why she treats him like this; pour a cup of coffee over her head; smash everything in sight; tell her exactly what she can do with the job.
- ask her if she does this to him because she has problems at home.
- tell her that he is aware of what she does and would like to know why.
- write her an anonymous letter telling her how he feels.
- go to his union representative about it.

- tell her that he is going to make an appointment with the managing director and that he is going to complain about her.
- ask his supervisor to speak to her.
- let her car tyres down.
- make anonymous telephone calls to her home in the middle of the night.
- ask to see the welfare officer.
- every time she criticises him, scream and faint.

These, and more, are all possibilities, though many would be immediately discounted. But imagining himself following up some of the more ridiculous solutions, even if it doesn't solve his problems, may make this person feel better and help him to put those problems into perspective. Of the more feasible suggestions, it might certainly be a good idea for him to go to his union representative or to ask the welfare officer for advice and help. He could ask his supervisor to talk to his boss, or confront her himself and tell her how he feels and ask her why she does it— both courses that would demand a great deal of courage, especially if he had to consider the possibility of being made redundant or dismissed.

Your client could try brainstorming with the following:

> 'I need to lose two stones in weight as soon as possible.'
> 'I can't stand my husband any longer.'
> 'I want to change my image.'
> 'I can't manage on the money I get.'
> 'I hate my wife's cooking.'

In each case his or her aim is to try to discover what possible solutions there might be, and how realistic and achievable they are. This takes us back to the skills of Stage 2. The client would look at each proposed solution, and ask:

> 'If I do this, what are the likely consequences for me and other people? What might happen?'

For and against   Having done his brainstorming exercise, the client writes down each possible course of action on a separate piece of paper. He divides each piece across the middle and writes 'for' in the top section and 'against' in the bottom one. Then he lists all the things he can think of that are for taking the action, and all those that militate against it.

Problem:

> 'Most of my work colleagues seem to ignore me and are often hostile, and this makes me unhappy at work. And I take this unhappiness home.'

Possible action:

> 'Try to be more open and friendly with colleagues.'

Points for:

- 'This might break through the barrier of unfriendliness.'
- 'It might improve relationships.'
- 'If it works I will be happier and, perhaps, so will they.'
- 'I don't like being unfriendly with them.'
- 'I won't be so miserable at home, and this should improve my relationships with my wife and children.'
- 'It seems a more human, rational and reasonable response.'
- 'My colleagues will see me in a different light.'

Points against:

- 'I would probably feel angry if I tried it because I would have to bury my feelings about what has happened.'
- 'It would not deal with my feelings about particular individuals.'
- 'How can I change the way I am and suddenly become friendly with a group who are hostile?'
- 'This solution suggests that the fault lies with me, and as far as I am aware I've not done anything to deserve the way they treat me.'

- 'I would feel rejected, hurt and stupid if it didn't work.'
- 'Some are friendly with me, so why don't I just stick with them and ignore the rest? I don't know why they do it so it's their problem, not mine.'
- 'Why am I making such a fuss about a few stupid and unfriendly people. It's all getting out of proportion. I don't need to change—they do.'

Looking at all of these comments, it seems that the reasons for and against do not deal with the overriding emotions. There are strong feelings of anger in general, and against some in particular. It would probably be necessary in the session to look more closely at these feelings and allow them to be expressed. Other things might emerge that have not yet been exposed or examined. Also, as trying to be more open and friendly doesn't seem acceptable, other methods of dealing with the problem would need to be looked at:

'I could not be nice to these people when they have treated me like this. I need another possible solution.'

Other possible solutions would be dealt with in the same way—brainstorming, then listing points for and against and weighing them all up.

(b) Force-field analysis

This is another method of looking at the pros and cons of a possible course of action, and is similar to the for-and-against approach. The idea is that with any possible course of action there will be forces around that pull the speaker in the direction of wanting to pursue it, and other forces that will pull him the other way and prevent him from doing it. Looking at these may help him to balance out the merits, or otherwise, of this particular action.

So the speaker makes a statement about what he would like to achieve, and then lists (1) those things that would prevent or hinder him from achieving it; and (2) those things that would help him achieve it. He then works out ways in which he can increase the forces that help and decrease the forces that prevent him from moving ahead. Take this goal as an example:

'I want to change my job.'

Forces that the speaker considers would *hinder*:

- 'There are few jobs around, and many people are looking for work.'
- 'I don't want to be one of the many unemployed because I would feel useless, and my wife would probably resent my being unemployed and at home, especially when she has a job.'
- 'I have a mortgage, and we couldn't manage financially if I resigned. If we had to sell our house and move, my wife wouldn't like it as she is happy where we are and we live near to her work.'
- 'I don't have many qualifications.'
- 'I don't like my work, but I can put up with it for the present.'
- 'I am afraid to do it.'
- 'I have many friends at work and would be sad to leave them.'
- 'The effect on the children would be substantial. They might have to move schools and change friends.'

Forces that the speaker thinks would *help*:

- 'I am not unhappy, but feel that I am not fulfilling my potential and would really like a different kind of work.'
- 'I would really like to be a teacher. That's my ambition.'
- 'My wife wouldn't be too happy, but I think she would support me.'
- 'There is a teacher-training course at the local college. I might get in as a mature student and I might be entitled to a grant.'

Examine each of the forces listed above. There seem to be positive points on both sides, but the main problems for your client appear to be:

1 'Would my wife support me, and how would it affect the relationship if I were to become a student at my age?'
2 'Could we manage financially without moving, and would I get a grant?'

Both of these would need some exploration. He could talk to his wife, and find out from the college what his position would be. Would he qualify as a mature student, and would he get a grant? These actions would increase the positive and decrease the negative forces. He would not yet have made a definite decision, but he would have begun to explore the possibilities, to take steps along the road to achieving his aim of becoming a teacher. The college might say that he doesn't have the necessary qualifications, and suggest training courses in order to achieve them; or they might accept him as a mature student. He might be entitled to a grant from various sources, about which the college could give advice. If a grant was not available, he couldn't pursue his aim at all without major changes in his, his wife's, and their children's lives.

Force-field analysis can help not just to decide on the best course of action, but to look at each option in turn with a view to increasing or decreasing the forces at work.

2 Changing behaviour
Changing a person's behaviour is often very difficult, and some would think that the services of a psychologist or psychiatrist would be necessary. In some cases this is true, but a non-professional listener can help people to look at possible courses of action and, sometimes, to discover the strength or courage in themselves to know what to do and to be able to do it. But, as we have noted, courses of action must be within the individual's capacity to carry them out. It is no use his deciding to confront his boss with her

behaviour if he is too frightened to do it, either because he might lose his job or because he just could not summon up the courage.

(a)   Rehearsing

One method of discovering the strength to act is through 'rehearsing'. This means that the person with the problem decides on the course of action and then talks and thinks it through in detail, perhaps writing down exactly what he would say. He can also do this by closing his eyes and imagining that he is doing it, and working through what he thinks might happen. He can rehearse with you, the listener, or do it at home in front of a mirror, or walk and talk through the process with someone else acting as the boss (or whoever it is who is at the centre of his problem) and responding in different ways.

The task of the listener is to help the other person to express his feelings, emotions and thoughts in ways that are appropriate both for him and for the situation. It would be of little use, even if it felt good at the time, for him to walk into the boss's office and scream and shout at her, unless of course he wanted to lose his job. One very positive side of listening is that, if a person has worked through Stages 1 and 2 in the listening process and has moved on to Stage 3, it could be that he has already acquired some kind of new strength within himself. If he has explored his problems and his life, has come to some new understanding and has started to look at possible solutions and goals, he may also have developed a new confidence in himself and in his own abilities and potential. This might enable him to do something that he could not have done before. The listening process helps him to do this. What must not happen is for you, the listener, to tell your client what to do:

'You think that you couldn't go to your boss and ask her about why she treats you like dirt? I think you could and should. It's only a matter of doing it, and you would

manage. You don't think you have the courage, but you
are stronger than you think.'

This is not encouragement, but a kind of blackmail, almost
bullying. It is advice-giving, and it is not helpful. The
decision to act must be the client's, something he feels able
to do, even if it does take some effort. And in order to act,
the client may have to learn to be more assertive.

As we noted earlier, assertiveness involves knowing,
believing in, stating and standing up for your own rights. It
is not the same as aggression, which usually means bull-
dozing over and into someone else's life and rights. Some
typical non-assertive statements:

'I don't have any rights of my own.'
'You should always put other people first.'
'You should never make mistakes.'
'You should always respect other people, especially those
in positions of authority.'
'You should never look for compliments.'
'You must never express how you feel, but should always
keep your feelings to yourself.'
'You should always take criticism—the critics may be
right.'
'You should never be angry, for anger can destroy you
and others.'
'You should always be self-sufficient.'
'You should always say "yes" when you can.'

The assertive opposites of these are:

'You have as many rights as other people.'
'You have a right to put yourself first sometimes.'
'Everybody makes mistakes—it is normal, and all people
are fallible and human and you have the right to make
mistakes sometimes.'
'Other people have to earn respect, especially those in
authority, and you have the right to disagree and have
your own opinions.'

'You have a right to be told when you have done something well.'
'You have a right to express how you feel.'
'You have a right to reject unfair criticism.'
'You have a right to express your anger.'
'You have a right to the support and help of others.'
'You have a right to say "no" when you want to.'

Obviously the appropriateness, or otherwise, of these statements will depend on the circumstances, but often people do feel and believe that they should not 'rock the boat' or 'make waves' in case it should upset others. Sometimes others *need* to be upset, though. Many people have a low self-image and poor self-esteem, and are too willing to let others ride over them. Any of the above statements, both the non-assertive and the assertive, could be the subjects of the listening process, and clients could be helped to examine them and work through them in the light of the context in which they arise.

Once the individual has decided on a course of action, he will probably need further support from you, the listener, and will need to feel that he can come back to you afterwards to let you know how he coped and what happened.

(b)   Role-changing
The process of changing behaviour can also be tackled by the listener and speaker assuming different roles within the scenario. In the case of confronting the boss with her behaviour, mentioned above, you, the listener, would become the client and the client the boss. You would then work through the encounter, using different approaches and responses. This would enable the client to see how you handle the problem, what you say and what you do—which might then enable him to use you as a role model and to copy your style and approach. When you have rehearsed these different roles, the client can change back to being himself and you become the boss, and both of you then

work through the action again. Finally, you comment on how the client has been coping and make any necessary remarks to affirm appropriate behaviour.

Having the courage to confront someone with her behaviour, and acting in a way that is 'out-of-character' in order to do it, is not easy. But this is not to say that an individual cannot learn new behaviour. One of the objects of the listening process is to help him to make choices and, having made them, to find or learn the best way of carrying out his decisions.

It will also help if the client is able to plan how and when he will take the action he has decided upon.

In the above case, it would probably be inappropriate for the client to go to see the boss at certain times: when she is very busy, when she is getting ready to go to a meeting or going home, when it is clear that she is not in a good mood or has some difficult decisions to make; when she has just had bad news or is tired and angry. It would be equally inappropriate for the client to go when the time is not right for *him*: when he is angry and upset; when he is unwell; when he is feeling unsure. Sometimes it helps if the plan of campaign is written down—it then becomes more concrete as a course of action.

3 Evaluating the costs and consequences
Evaluation can be carried out before and after any action has been taken.

Beforehand, the possible solutions, choices and decisions can be examined and the costs and consequences evaluated:

'If I do this rather than that, how will it affect me, my boss, my colleagues, my partner, my wife, my husband, my children . . .?'
'How helpful do I think this is likely to be to me and to others?'
'What might be the likely consequences for me and for others?'

'What will it cost in terms of my job, my relationships, my self-esteem, my financial position, my emotions?'
'What will it cost others?'

In the case of someone unhappy at work and wishing to leave, what are the possible consequences for him and his family? If he leaves work, what might happen?

'If I decide to leave work, how will this affect me, my wife, the children, our friends and family?'
'Will I be able to get another job?'
'What will the financial costs be and how much would we have to live on? What about the mortgage?'
'What will the consequences be for me and for everyone involved?'

Asking questions like these can give some indication of whether or not the action is realistic or possible under the circumstances, and how it might work out. It is part of the process of exploring goals, finding solutions and making choices. Once a decision has been made and the action has been taken, the client may usefully ask questions such as:

'Was it worth it, and how did it work out?'
'Did it work out as I expected or wanted?'
'Was it a good or positive outcome for me?
'Did I get it wrong and stray from what I had decided to do? If I did, in what ways?'
'How did it affect the other person or persons involved? How did they react, and what did they say and do?'
'Do I need to do it again, and if so, how?'
'Do I need to look at other ways of achieving the same goal?'
'Should I go back and look at the possible goals and solutions again, and re-evaluate both my position and my choices?'

It is useful to look at what resources are available to help in making and carrying out decisions. These could come from a number of different sources, ranging from close family members to people within the organisation that the individual works for, outsiders and professionals:

* wife, husband, partner, brother, sister, parent
* colleague, friend, neighbour, associate
* supervisor, welfare officer, personnel manager, occupational health nurse, doctor, clergyman, social worker, solicitor, lawyer
* Citizens' Advice Bureaux, Relate, Cruse, social services, equal opportunities organisations, employment agency

The personal and inner resources of the client also need to be considered—in fact, these will have been relevant throughout the listening process when considering the appropriate information to be given; when looking at problems, goals and decisions; and when considering possible courses of action and the assertiveness and courage necessary to carry them out.

4 Endings

Endings are important, for this is not simply a matter of client and listener just getting up and saying 'Goodbye'. In terms of listening skills, you, the listener, have succeeded when you are no longer needed and your client is able to make and carry out his own decisions. Remember that his decision may be to do nothing, to make no new decisions at all. But if the client does decide to stay exactly where he is, this may be as valid a decision as any.

There are three main kinds of endings:

(a) *Happy endings* An ending is usually happy when the client:

* takes action—accepts his or her own decisions and can find the courage to carry them out;
* does nothing—is happy for things to remain unchanged;
* is not dependent on you, the listener—has become independent;

- accepts referral—knows where to go for help;
- acknowledges support—knows that you are available if necessary.

Usually, the ending is happy when some acceptable and possible solutions have been achieved.

(b)   *Unhappy endings*   An unhappy ending is one that is unsatisfactory for either the client or the listener, or both—

The client:
- is passive—he is unable to do anything or make any decisions (he may also be annoyed, disillusioned or apathetic);
- is dissatisfied—he expresses some kind of discontent, or is silent, hostile or aggressive;
- feels rejected—he feels that the listener has not understood.

You, the listener:

- are assertive—you are dominating;
- are dissatisfied—you are discontented, silent, hostile, aggressive, angry or apathetic;
- feel rejected—you are unable to do anything and feel that you are useless.

Any of these situations might arise because you, the listener, have not listened properly and have not used the skills in the right way; or because your client found it so difficult or painful that he refused or has been unable to work at his problems.

(c)   *Neutral endings*   Here the client or the listener, or both, feel that the session has been a waste of time because nothing seems to have come out of it. They separate, feeling that it was all rather pointless.

Learning as you end
When a session takes place within a certain time frame,

such as an hour, it is usual to leave some time at the end for appraisal, for looking at what has happened during that time. (Appraisal should also be carried out at the end of a series of sessions.) It can be done by general discussion, or by either the client or both client and listener writing down and then discussing answers to certain questions.

Before acting, your client should ask:

- 'What have I learned from this session?'
- 'In what ways has it changed me?'
- 'In what ways has it changed my situation?'
- 'What decisions has it helped me to make?'
- 'How do I feel about these decisions, and am I capable of carrying them out?'

After acting, he should ask:

- 'What happened when I took the action decided upon, and what is the result now? Did it work, and how?"
- 'How did my decisions and actions affect others?'
- 'How do I feel about it now?'
- 'What are the positive elements, and what have I achieved or gained?'
- 'Has it been negative, and have I lost anything?'

At the end, where appropriate, you should make the offer of a further session, telling your client that he may, if he wants to, come back again (or make contact in some other way):

'If you wish to do so, I am always available to see you. Just let me know, and we can make an appointment.'

'Come back and see me and let me know how things have worked out for you. I would be interested to hear from you and see you again.'

'Thank you for coming. It was good to see you, and if you wish to come back again I am always available.'

Some would close by shaking hands and saying, 'Goodbye'.

The coping listener

It is useful for you, the listener, to spend some time afterwards looking at what has happened in a session and at what was achieved. This can be done alone and, if you want to, by making and keeping confidential notes. Those who listen to others find that it requires a great deal of energy and concentration, and that they carry something of this away with them into their own lives. It is especially the case when problems are distressing and disturbing. Any good listener who displays the skills of active listening will find that she needs to some extent to offload the problems and emotions that she has absorbed from others. She may also discover that some of her own personal feelings and problems, from the past or from the present, have been resurrected. These can influence her own stress level and affect her in a number of ways, both at work and at home. She will find that she copes better when she is able to talk to someone about what has happened, and about how she feels and has reacted. This can be more usefully done with someone who is neutral, as long as confidentiality is maintained. Whereas the professional counsellor will be under supervision, the non-professional listener and helper's support can come from a colleague or senior, or from someone outside the organisation. Without such support, listeners may become clients!

12 Referral

It is necessary for those involved in helping and listening to know where they can refer people who come to them. This is rather like the final part of Stage 3 of listening skills, where the concern is with action and the future. The possible resources available are personal, group, organisational and external.

1 Personal
Here you, the listener, consider sources of help from within your client's own circle. Help may be available from the family—from a partner, parent, brother or sister—or from a friend or a colleague at work. It is a matter of asking the client where she thinks the best source of help for her is:

Who can she talk to, either inside or outside work, about her problems, and who will try to listen and understand?

Some feel unable to share their problems with their partner, believing that they would not be offered support or understanding from that quarter:

So is there someone else she feels she can trust at work, or from within her immediate circle of family and friends?

2 Group
If the individual with the problem is a member of a team or group, it is likely that there will be at least one other person within that team who is a special friend or colleague—someone he can talk to, and trust. This kind of

help is particularly likely to be available at work. Or the potential confidant may be a neighbour or friend that he sees regularly and so is likely to be able to provide support outside work. For some problems, the whole team or group may give support—through understanding and caring, through a sense of solidarity and a shared feeling of belonging, and by just being there when needed.

3 Organisational
Managers, supervisors and colleagues should show what facilities are available for help, advice and counselling at work and via the organisation. In any particular workplace, there are probably some, if not all, of the following: a personnel officer, a welfare officer, an occupational health department or nurse, a consultant medical officer, a health and safety officer, a union official, counsellors, a consultant psychiatrist, a consultant psychologist and financial consultants.

Sometimes personnel officers, welfare officers and occupational health nurses are trained in counselling. In any event, they should all be good listeners and able to offer help and advice on a wide range of matters. Larger organisations employ counsellors full-time, and some have counsellors available part-time, privately or from outside agencies. Occupational health departments deal with health-related matters, but this almost always includes personal and welfare problems too. Medical officers, psychiatrists and psychologists may be available through the occupational health department nurse, and for most practical and general matters a union representative can probably be called in. Many organisations have employee assistance programmes, EAPs, through which help, advice and counselling can be obtained, usually through outside agencies.

4 External
Help may need to be sought from specialist outside agencies, and many will take personal referrals only—that

is, from the individuals concerned. As a listener, you need to know what agencies are available in your locality; you could probably get advice about these from departments in the workplace such as personnel, welfare and occupational health. The more commonly known ones are:

Relate	personal and marital problems
Catholic Marriage Advisory Council	personal and marital problems
Citizens' Advice Bureau	advice and help of any kind
Alcoholics Anonymous	alcohol-related problems
Cruse	bereavement
Compassionate Friends	bereavement
SANDS	bereavement—babies and children
SSAFA	general help for ex-Service personnel
Samaritans	help for those who feel they can't cope with life

For other organisations and addresses, see pages 256–7.

There are many local organisations and individuals that offer counselling help; their names can probably be obtained from the telephone directory or from the Citizens' Advice Bureau. Local GPs and social work departments often know of individuals and organisations that specialise in certain problems. Local priests and ministers are also a useful source of help, and many do not confine themselves to so-called 'religious' or 'spiritual' problems. Most are trained in listening and helping, and some may be trained counsellors.

For problems of redundancy and unemployment there are a number of organisations offering help and advice, and probably the first place to start is the Employment Department and Employment Service. There are also Jobcentres and advisory services giving advice about seminars, workshops, courses and training programmes.

The list of helping organisations, individuals and charities is almost endless, and the good listener will have extensive knowledge in this area.

One final problem is that some may not seek help, and furthermore, may not wish to be helped. Not to want help is, of course, anyone's basic right, but when they encounter this those who seek to listen and help can feel impotent, angry, frustrated and helpless. But we do not listen in order to solve other people's problems for them. In the end they have to make their own choices, no matter how limited, and find their own solutions in their own way.

SOME USEFUL ORGANISATIONS

ACAS (Advisory, Conciliation and Arbitration Service)
Has nine regional offices and can offer advice and help on all employment matters; produces leaflets and booklets on many different topics.

British Association for Counselling
1 Regent Place, Rugby, Warwickshire CV21 2PJ
Tel: 01788 550899
Includes the Association for Counselling at Work.

Citizens' Advice Bureaux (CAB)
Offices in most towns and cities, offering free advice on all matters.

Commission for Racial Equality
Elliot House, 10–12 Allington Street, London SW1E 5EH
Tel: 0171 828 7022
For those who feel they are being discriminated against on the grounds of race.

Equal Opportunities Commission
Overseas House, Quay Street, Manchester M3 3HN
Tel: 0161 833 9244
For those who feel that they are being discriminated against on the grounds of sex or race.

Labour Relations Agency
Windsor House, 9–15 Bedford Street, Belfast BT2 7NU
Tel: 01232 321442
For advice to employees and employers on any employment problem.

Lesbian and Gay Employment Rights (LAGER)
Tel: 0181 983 0696 (gay); 0181 983 0694 (lesbian)
For those who feel that they are being harassed because of their sexual orientation.

Rape Crisis Help Line
Tel: 0171 837 1600

Relate
Herbert Grey College, Little Church Street, Rugby,
Warwickshire CV21 3AP
Tel: 01788 573241

Rights of Women
52–4 Featherstone Street, London EC1Y 8RT
Tel: 0171 251 6577

WASH (Women Against Sexual Harassment)
242 Pentonville Road, London N1 9UN
Tel: 0171 837 7509

Further Reading

GENERAL LISTENING AND COUNSELLING

Berne, Eric, *Games People Play*, London: Penguin Books, 1966

Dainow, S. and Bailey, C., *Developing Skills with People*, Chichester: John Wiley and Sons, 1988

Jacobs, Michael, *Swift to Hear*, London: SPCK, 1985

Kennedy, E. and Charles, S.C., *On Becoming a Counsellor*, Dublin: Gill & Macmillan, rev. edn 1990

McKay, M., Davis, M. and Fanning, P., *Messages: The Communication Skills Book*, USA: New Harbinger Publications, 1985

Munro, E.A., Manthei, R.J. and Small, J.J., *Counselling: A Skills Approach*, New Zealand: Methuen, 1983

Nelson-Jones, R., *Practical Counselling Skills*, London: Holt Rinehart & Winston, 1983

Nelson-Jones, R., *Human Relationship Skills*, London: Cassell Educational, 1986

Pease, Alan, *Body Language*, London: Sheldon Press, 1984

Pincus, Lily, *Secrets in the Family*, London: Faber and Faber, 1978

Priestley, P. and McGuire, J., *Learning to Help*, London: Tavistock Publications, 1983

Skynner, R. and Cleese, J., *Families and How to Survive Them*, London: Methuen, 1987

Skynner, R. and Cleese, J., *Life and How to Survive It*, London: Methuen, 1993

Winnicott, D. W., *Playing and Reality*, London: Pelican Books, 1985

PSYCHOLOGY AND COUNSELLING

Berne, Eric, *A Layman's Guide to Psychiatry and Psycho-analysis*, London: Penguin Books, 1968

Harris, Thomas, *I'm OK—You're OK*, London: Pan Books, 1973

Jacobs, M., *The Presenting Past*, Milton Keynes: Open University Press, 1986

Jacobs, M., *Psychodynamic Counselling in Action*, London: Sage Publications, 1989

Mearns, D. and Thorne, B., *Person-centred Counselling in Action*, London: Sage Publications, 1988

STRESS

Atkinson, J. M., *Coping with Stress at Work*, London: Thorsons

Coleman, Vernon, *Overcoming Stress*, London: Sheldon Press

Consumer Publications, *Understanding Stress*, London: Hodder & Stoughton

Cooper, C., Cooper, R. and Eaker, L. *Living with Stress*, London: Penguin Books, 1988

Kirsta, A., *The Book of Stress Survival*, London: Unwin Paperbacks

Looker, T. and Gregson, O., *Stress Wise*, London: Hodder & Stoughton, 1989

REDUNDANCY

Allen, S., *The Experience of Unemployment*, London: Macmillan, 1986

Bainham, J. and Cox, D., *Job Hunting Made Easy*, London: Kogan Page, 1992

Bainton, C. and Crowley, T., *Beyond Redundancy*, London: Thorsons, 1992

Bolles, R. N., *What Colour Is Your Parachute?*, USA: Ten Speed Press, 1993

Corfield, R., *How You Can Get That Job*, London: Kogan Page, 1993

Doherty, N. and Tyson, S., *Executive Redundancy and Outplacement*, London: Kogan Page, 1993
Jackson, T., *Perfect Job Search Strategies*, London: Piatkus, 1994

Relevant publications may also be obtained from the Department of Social Security and the Employment Service Benefits Agency.

BEREAVEMENT AND LOSS
Collick, Elizabeth, *Through Grief*, London: Darton, Longman & Todd, 1987
Kubler-Ross, E., *On Death and Dying*, London: Tavistock, 1970
Lake, Tony, *Living with Grief*, London: Sheldon Press, 1984
Lewis, C. S., *A Grief Observed*, London: Faber and Faber, 1961
Murray-Parkes, Colin, *Bereavement*, London: Pelican Books, 1975
Pincus, Lily, *Death and the Family*, London: Faber and Faber, 1976
Raphael, Beverley, *The Anatomy of Bereavement*, London: Routledge, 1992
Whitaker, A., *All in the End Is Harvest: An Anthology for Those Who Grieve*, London: Darton, Longman & Todd, 1984
Worden, J. William, *Grief Counselling and Grief Therapy*, London: Routledge Tavistock: 1983

POST-TRAUMA STRESS
Bettelheim, B., *The Informed Heart*, London: Peregrine Books, 1986
Hodgkinson, P. and Stewart, M., *Coping with Catastrophe*, London: Routledge, 1991
Keenan, Brian, *An Evil Cradling*, London: Vintage Press, 1992

Parkinson, F. W., *Post-trauma Stress*, London: Sheldon Press, 1993

Scott, M. J. and Stradling, S. G., *Counselling for Post-traumatic Stress Disorder*, London: Sage Publications, 1992

SEX, SEXUAL HARASSMENT AND BULLYING

Adams, A., *Bullying at Work*, London: Virago Press, 1992

Brown, P. and Faulder, C., *Treat Yourself to Sex*, London: Penguin Books, 1977

Curtis, L., *Sexual Harassment at Work: How to Cope*, London: BBC Publications, 1993

Hadjifotiou, N., *Women and Harassment at Work*, London: Pluto Press, 1984

Litvinoff, S., *The Relate Guide to Sex*, London: Vermilion, 1992

Wise, Sue, *Georgie Porgie: Sexual Harassment in Everyday Life*, London: Pandora Press, 1987

MARRIAGE AND MARITAL RELATIONSHIPS

Dominian, J., *Make or Break*, London: SPCK, 1984

Gough, Tony, *Couples Arguing*, London: Darton, Longman & Todd, 1987

Gough, Tony, *Couples in Counselling*, London: Darton, Longman & Todd, 1989

James, A. L. and Wilson, K., *Couples, Conflict and Change*, London: Tavistock, 1986

Scarf, Maggie, *Intimate Partners*, New York: Random House, 1987

ALCOHOL, DRUGS AND SUBSTANCE ABUSE

Schilit, R. and Lisansky, E. S., *Drugs and Behaviour*, London: Sage Publications, 1994

Velleman, R., *Counselling for Alcohol Problems*, London: Sage Publications, 1994

GENERAL INTEREST

Marks, I. M., *Living with Fear*, London: McGraw Hill, 1980

Rowe, D., *Beyond Fear*, London: Fontana, 1987

Rowe, D., *Choosing, Not Losing: The Experience of Depression*, London: Fontana, 1988

Rowe, D., *Breaking the Bonds: Understanding Depression, Finding Freedom*, London: Fontana, 1991

Weekes, Claire, *Peace from Nervous Suffering*, London: Angus & Robertson, 1972

Weekes, Claire, *Self-Help for Your Nerves*, London: Angus & Robertson, 1988

Some of the above books are expensive, but could be kept in a small reference library. Some may now be out of print, but can be obtained from a public library.

Index